Contents

Introduction

There is no doubt about it: A gift that you have made yourself is the very best way to show how much you care. Here is a selection of *Beautiful Patchwork Presents* that you can make for the special people in your life.

The projects are divided into 5 categories: babies and children, women, men, the home and Christmas. By leafing through these sections, you will almost certainly find something to make that will satisfy all your gift-giving needs, whether it be a birthday, a wedding or anniversary, the birth of a new child, Mother's Day, Father's Day, Christmas, or any other holiday throughout the year.

Many of the projects are very quick to make, such as the Patchwork Bibs, Circular Patchwork Pictures, House Cushion and Christmas Tree Ornaments. Others, such as the Harlequin Wall Hanging, Maple Leaf Quilt and Ribbons & Bows Tablecloth, are more time-consuming. It is up to you to decide how much time you can give to a project, and how small or large, simple or complex it should be. Each of the 5 gift categories will provide you with an interesting and varied selection of patchwork presents from which to choose.

Beautiful Patchwork Presents is divided into a chapter explaining techniques, a chapter of block designs, and a projects chapter. Begin by studying the first chapter, *Making Patchwork Projects: Techniques*, very carefully. This chapter gives instructions on how to cut and piece patchwork, how to quilt and then how to finish a project. I will refer to the techniques in this chapter throughout the book, so if you familiarize yourself very thoroughly with this material, it will be easy for you to look back and find the technique under discussion. For example, if a block design requires insetting or sewing curves, I will refer you to the section that tells you how to do

it: *How to Inset* or *Sewing Curves*. When it comes time to quilt, you'll be referred to *How to Quilt* where you'll find a discussion on hand and machine quilting, as well as tufting and quilt-as-you-go techniques—all with clear illustrations. If you need to finish a project with binding, I'll refer you to *Binding a Project*. If you can't remember exactly where these techniques are found, you can look up the page number in the *Index* at the back of the book.

The next chapter consists of block designs in 2 sizes. *Block Designs* contains 24 distinctive designs for patchwork blocks and tiny traditional designs. All the block designs are rated as easy, moderate or challenging, and all include 2 assembly diagrams and full-size templates. The 10-inch-square designs are accompanied by written directions; you can construct the 2-inch-square designs by following the exploded assembly diagrams which guide you in the order in which to sew the seams. While some of the designs are familiar, many of the 10-inch-square designs are new—published here for the first time. From these block designs you can create many different projects which are featured in the third chapter, *Beautiful Patchwork Gifts*.

The third chapter is divided into 5 sections: *Gifts for Babies and Children, Presents for Women, Mementos for Men, Treasures for the Home* and *Christmas Presents*. You'll find dozens of appealing items to make for yourself, or for your family and friends. These designs are based on the 10-inch square or 2-inch square or are self-contained. Whichever project you choose, however, you'll find complete instructions along with assembly diagrams and full-size templates, enabling you to make your chosen project with ease. Color photographs of all the projects will provide you with inspiration about possible fabric choices.

METRIC EQUIVALENCY CHART

MM—MILLIMETRES   CM—CENTIMETRES

INCHES TO MILLIMETRES AND CENTIMETRES

INCHES	MM	CM	INCHES	CM	INCHES	CM
1/8	3	0.3	9	22.9	30	76.2
1/4	6	0.6	10	25.4	31	78.7
3/8	10	1.0	11	27.9	32	81.3
1/2	13	1.3	12	30.5	33	83.8
5/8	16	1.6	13	33.0	34	86.4
3/4	19	1.9	14	35.6	35	88.9
7/8	22	2.2	15	38.1	36	91.4
1	25	2.5	16	40.6	37	94.0
1 1/4	32	3.2	17	43.2	38	96.5
1 1/2	38	3.8	18	45.7	39	99.1
1 3/4	44	4.4	19	48.3	40	101.6
2	51	5.1	20	50.8	41	104.1
2 1/2	64	6.4	21	53.3	42	106.7
3	76	7.6	22	55.9	43	109.2
3 1/2	89	8.9	23	58.4	44	111.8
4	102	10.2	24	61.0	45	114.3
4 1/2	114	11.4	25	63.5	46	116.8
5	127	12.7	26	66.0	47	119.4
6	152	15.2	27	68.6	48	121.9
7	178	17.8	28	71.1	49	124.5
8	203	20.3	29	73.7	50	127.0

YARDS TO METRES

YARDS	METRES	YARDS	METRES	YARDS	METRES	YARDS	METRES	YARDS	METRES
1/8	0.11	2 1/8	1.94	4 1/8	3.77	6 1/8	5.60	8 1/8	7.43
1/4	0.23	2 1/4	2.06	4 1/4	3.89	6 1/4	5.72	8 1/4	7.54
3/8	0.34	2 3/8	2.17	4 3/8	4.00	6 3/8	5.83	8 3/8	7.66
1/2	0.46	2 1/2	2.29	4 1/2	4.11	6 1/2	5.94	8 1/2	7.77
5/8	0.57	2 5/8	2.40	4 5/8	4.23	6 5/8	6.06	8 5/8	7.89
3/4	0.69	2 3/4	2.51	4 3/4	4.34	6 3/4	6.17	8 3/4	8.00
7/8	0.80	2 7/8	2.63	4 7/8	4.46	6 7/8	6.29	8 7/8	8.12
1	0.91	3	2.74	5	4.57	7	6.40	9	8.23
1 1/8	1.03	3 1/8	2.86	5 1/8	4.69	7 1/8	6.52	9 1/8	8.34
1 1/4	1.14	3 1/4	2.97	5 1/4	4.80	7 1/4	6.63	9 1/4	8.46
1 3/8	1.26	3 3/8	3.09	5 3/8	4.91	7 3/8	6.74	9 3/8	8.57
1 1/2	1.37	3 1/2	3.20	5 1/2	5.03	7 1/2	6.86	9 1/2	8.69
1 5/8	1.49	3 5/8	3.31	5 5/8	5.14	7 5/8	6.97	9 5/8	8.80
1 3/4	1.60	3 3/4	3.43	5 3/4	5.26	7 3/4	7.09	9 3/4	8.92
1 7/8	1.71	3 7/8	3.54	5 7/8	5.37	7 7/8	7.20	9 7/8	9.03
2	1.83	4	3.66	6	5.49	8	7.32	10	9.14

Making Patchwork Projects: Techniques

Selecting Fabrics & Threads

Each design is accompanied by a screened illustration, an assembly diagram, and a list of templates that tells you how many pieces are needed and their suggested color or value (degree of light or dark): white, light, bright, medium, dark. Bright fabrics can be any color or shade; they are meant to add a flash of unusual or startling color to add spice to the designs. Sometimes, I suggest the word "sky" or "striped" to indicate a color; it is up to you to select a suitable fabric. Follow the template lists, diagrams and illustrations exactly, or experiment with the placement of colors to create your own interpretation of each design.

Fabrics woven from 100-percent cotton threads are best for quiltmaking, although fabrics with some polyester content can be used. Don't use anything with less than 70-percent cotton, however. Select fabrics with highly contrasting values. Unorthodox combinations are fine and fun to use—especially in a small project. Select an attractive interplay of solid fabrics (or fabrics with a tiny all-over print), fabrics with a medium-scale print and at least one with a large-scale print.

Because of the small size of many of the projects in this book, it won't always be necessary to purchase new fabric. In many cases, only a few scraps are needed to complete an entire project. Check your rag bag before buying new fabrics. You may find that this book will enable you to finally use up all those old materials that have been haunting you, thus giving you lots of room (and an excuse) to buy new fabrics!

If you are buying new fabrics, try to buy all fabrics for your project at the same time. You can best see how colors and patterns work with one another while they are still on the bolt. Matching fabrics from small scraps is very difficult and quite often doesn't work when you take the new selections home.

If in doubt about yardages, always buy *more* fabric than you think you'll need. Dye lots vary considerably; often, by the time you realize that you'll need more fabric, it may be too late to find the same dye lot with the exact same color. The fabric yardages listed for each project are exact and assume your cutting is precise. If you're not sure about the accuracy of your cutting, buy a little more fabric—you can always use the leftover pieces in some future creation.

When you are satisfied with your fabric choices, buy your sewing thread—an unobtrusive color that will blend with all the fabrics.

Washing & Straightening

Prewash all fabrics to be used in your project. Wash fabrics of a similar color in the very hottest water and hang them to dry (tangling in a clothes dryer can twist the fabrics off-grain). To wash scraps, place similar colors in a net bag before putting in the machine—this will eliminate much of the inevitable fraying that occurs. Before putting new fabrics in the washing machine, clip into the selvages (finished edges) at 2-inch intervals to accommodate shrinkage. If there is any evidence that the fabric is not colorfast (the colors will bleed), wash the fabric again, or soak it in a solution of 3 parts cold water and 1 part white vinegar. Rinse the fabric and spread it on a white towel while wet. If there is still evidence of color bleeding, discard the fabric and select another. It is better to make this effort in the beginning than to experience the horror of washing a finished project only to find that it has been ruined by bleeding fabrics. If possible, iron the fabrics while they are slightly damp; the dampness makes it easier to remove all the wrinkles. Trim away any frayed edges.

Check the grain. The crosswise and lengthwise threads of the fabric should be exactly perpendicular to each other. If they aren't perpendicular grasp the four corners of the fabric and pull diagonally from opposite corners simultaneously to straighten the grain (this is better done with two pairs of hands). Repeat this, pulling alternately from opposite corners until the threads are perpendicular to one another.

Prepare the fabrics for cutting as follows: Accurately cut off any selvages or uneven edges. To do this, measure an even distance from each edge (selvages are usually ¼ inch but can be as wide as ½ inch); draw a cutting line with a pencil and ruler. Cut away the edges along the pencil line. Next, using a triangle and a ruler, draw a line across the fabric that is exactly perpendicular to the cut edge (Fig. 1). Cut away any excess fabric beyond this line. You are now ready to make your templates, mark your fabric and cut out your pieces.

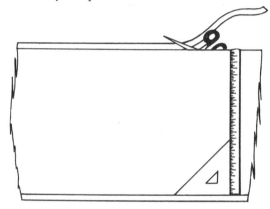

Fig. 1   Cutting away the selvages

Making Templates & Cutting the Pieces

Using tracing paper and a pencil, trace the templates for the designs you have chosen. Mark each tracing with the name of the design, the letter of the template (the letter "I" is not used for templates in this book) and the value(s) of the fabric(s) from which it should be cut.

Glue the tracing to medium-weight cardboard or plastic; allow the glue to dry. Cut out each template using a utility knife or other cutting blade. For straight lines, use a straight metal edge to guide the knife.

The edge of the template is the sewing line; therefore, a ¼-inch seam allowance *must be added* when marking the templates on the fabric. The best way to do this is by drawing a ¼-inch seam allowance on the wrong side of the fabric along the lengthwise and crosswise cut edges (Fig. 2). You can then place the edge of your template on the marked line. Trace around the edge of your template. Use a ruler to mark a ¼-inch seam allowance around each of the remaining edges before marking the next template. Continue to mark all your templates on the wrong side of the fabric in this way.

To avoid waste and conserve fabric, mark your pieces so that they can be cut along a mutual edge (Fig. 3 and Fig. 4). As a rule, the longest edge of any template should be placed on the straight (lengthwise) grain of the fabric. *All* edges of squares and rectangles should be on the straight grain.

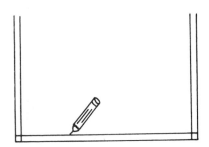

Fig. 2

Follow the list given with each design for the number of pieces to be cut and how to cut them. Symmetrical pieces do not need to be flipped over or "reversed," but many of the designs are made up of asymmetrical pieces; thus their mirror image or reverse side is needed to complete a pattern. This need to reverse is always indicated with each list. When a design is asymmetrical and you are not instructed to reverse the template, it means the template has already been reversed for you. Where the list indicates a number of pieces are "reversed," flip your template over and mark the necessary number of pieces on the fabric. You can check your work by studying the assembly diagram for your block.

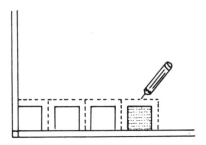

Fig. 3

After you have marked your pieces, carefully cut them out along the cutting lines. *Accuracy*—in both marking and cutting—is essential to the successful completion of each project. If you are cutting out all of your pieces at once, carefully gather and keep the pieces for each project in a separate envelope or plastic bag to avoid confusion when sewing time arrives.

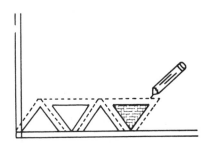

Fig. 4

Rotary Cutting

A few years ago I was introduced to the rotary cutter, which forever changed my outlook on cutting out patchwork pieces for certain projects. Using a rotary cutter for simple shapes—strips, squares, rectangles, and triangles—will halve the amount of time you spend on a project. The secret lies in cutting several layers at the same time.

Only 3 pieces of equipment are required for ro-

tary cutting, and while the initial expense may be more than you might wish to spend, the saving in time and the unbelievable accuracy you'll achieve will more than make up for what you pay. You'll need a rotary cutter with a *large* wheel, a cutting board specially designed for a rotary cutter, and a thick plastic ruler with marked grid or cutting lines. These items can be found in any well-stocked quilt-

9

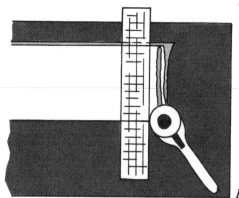

Fig. 5

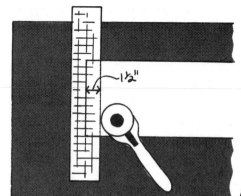

Fig. 6

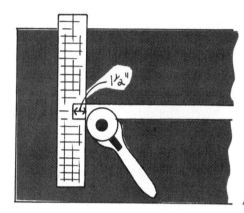

Fig. 7

ing shop. The cutting board can also be found in most art supply shops; ask for the "self-healing" type.

About 4–6 layers of material can be cut at one time, depending upon the fabric weight. Beginners should work with 4 layers. To prepare the fabric, fold in half on the straight grain with selvages matching, and steam-press. Fold in half again, creating 4 layers, and press again. Without unfolding it, place the fabric on the cutting board; then place your ruler on the fabric, aligning one of the grid lines with the pressed folded edge. Holding the ruler firmly on the fabric, run the blade of the rotary cutter along the edge of the ruler; this will cut away any ragged edges and straighten your fabric on grain (Fig. 5). Always push the blade *away* from you when cutting fabrics.

You are now ready to cut strips. Decide upon the width of the strips you require; then add ½ inch for seam allowances. For example, if your project requires 1-inch strips, your strip will need to be 1½

inches to accommodate the ¼-inch seam allowances at each edge. (For ease in cutting for right-handed quilters, move the fabric so that your straight outer edge is at the left of the cutting board; left-handed quilters should reverse these instructions.) Position the ruler on the fabric so that your cutting edge is 1½ inches away from the outer edge of the fabric (Fig. 6). Run the blade of your rotary cutter along the edge of the ruler to cut the strip. To cut squares, trim one edge of the strip to remove the folds. Turn the strip and measure 1½ inches away from the cut end; cut along this measurement and you'll have 4 perfect squares (Fig. 7). If you measure correctly and cut firmly, your squares will be extremely accurate without having to use a template!

Strips, such as those used for the Christmas Stocking or for Seminole Patchwork are cut in seconds using a rotary cutter. Save any leftover strips in a bag for a future scrap project. Try this technique and you'll never cut strips or other simple shapes with scissors again!

Sewing the Pieces: Patchwork

I assume you will use a sewing machine to sew the pieces for each project, although it is perfectly acceptable (though much slower) to do the piecing by hand.

Each design is accompanied by complete piecing instructions. Most designs are assembled in sub-units (squares, triangles, strips) that are then joined to complete the design.

When sewing pieces together, match the raw edges carefully, pinning them together at each end if

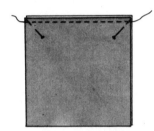

Fig. 8

necessary (Fig. 8). Sew the pieces together in chains to save time (Fig. 9). Always press the seams to one side, preferably towards the darker fabric (Fig. 10).

Fig. 9

When sewing sub-units together, carefully match the seams before you sew, pinning the pieces at crucial points (Fig. 11). When matching seams, it is best to press seam allowances in opposite directions.

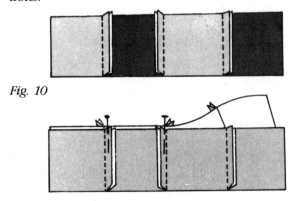

Fig. 10

Fig. 11

HOW TO INSET

Sometimes, pieces of a design must be inset into one another. While this procedure is slightly tricky at first, it is possible to get perfect corners every time by using the following method:

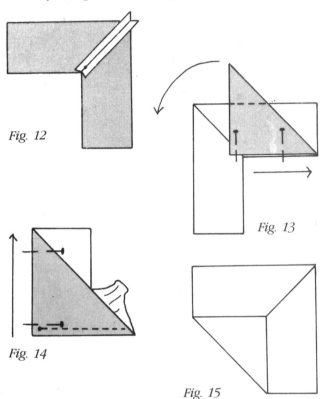

Fig. 12

Fig. 13

Fig. 14

Fig. 15

1. A triangular or square piece is inset into two other pieces that are sewn together to form an angle (Fig. 12). When sewing the pieces that form the angle together, end your stitching ¼ inch away from the edge to be inset (shown by the dot in the diagram).

2. Pin the piece to be inset along one edge of the angle (Fig. 13) and stitch from the middle (dot) to the edge (in the direction of the arrow).

3. Folding the excess fabric out of the way, pin the unsewn edges together and stitch from the central point to the outer edge (Fig. 14).

4. Open out the fabrics and carefully steam-press (Fig. 15). If you notice any puckers at the corner, you can usually eliminate them by removing a stitch from one of the seams just sewn.

SEWING CURVES

Curved edges are time-consuming to sew, but quite rewarding when finished. Excellent results can be achieved by following this procedure:

1. Cut both pieces so that the curved edges are on the bias. Mark the seam allowances on the wrong side; also mark dots for matching the curved edges (Fig. 16).

2. Pin the pieces together matching the dots and side edges. Use as many pins as necessary, easing the bias edges to fit (Fig. 17).

3. Open out the fabrics and steam-press carefully (Fig. 18).

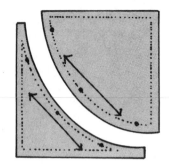

Fig. 16

HOW TO APPLIQUÉ

"Appliqué" means to apply to a larger surface, or in this technique, to sew one piece of fabric over another. While this book mainly features patchwork (or pieced) designs, there are some examples that require small decorative touches to be appliquéd in place. Hand appliqué is recommended.

Press the seam allowance ¼ inch to the wrong side and baste in place, if desired.

Place the pressed appliqué in its correct position on your patchwork. Slipstitch in place, using tiny invisible stitches. Backstitch at the end to secure your thread.

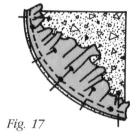

Fig. 17

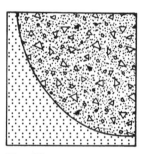

Fig. 18

Special Techniques

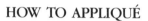

You can use special techniques to enhance or finish a project; these are referred to throughout the book.

RUFFLE

Cut a fabric strip to the required size, piecing the strip, if necessary, for additional length. With right sides together, stitch the short ends to each other (Fig. 19), forming a continuous circle of fabric. Fold the fabric in half lengthwise with wrong sides together and press; machine-baste ¼ inch away from the raw edges all around (Fig. 20). Gently pull the basting stitches, gathering the ruffle to approximately fit the edges of the project (Fig. 21). With raw edges even, pin the ruffle to the right side of the project, adjusting the gathers evenly to fit; allow ex-

tra gathers or make a pleat at each of the corners (Fig. 22). Stitch the ruffle securely to the project.

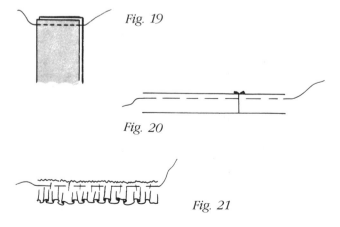

Fig. 19

Fig. 20

Fig. 21

LACE

With raw edges even, pin the lace to the right side of the project; allow extra gathers or make a pleat at each of the corners (Fig. 22). Overlap the beginning and end of the lace by about ¼ inch; then stitch the lace securely to the project.

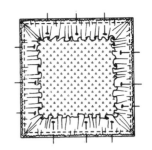

Fig. 22

PIPING

Cut the fabric strip to the required size, piecing the strip, if necessary, to achieve the proper length. Place the piping cord on the middle of the wrong side of the fabric; then fold the fabric in half lengthwise, enclosing the piping cord. Using a zipper foot on the sewing machine, stitch close to the cord (Fig. 23). Trim the seam allowance to ¼ inch. Pin the piping to the right side of the project with raw edges even. To ease the piping around each corner, clip into the seam allowance to the stitching line (Fig. 24). Continue pinning the piping in place until you reach the beginning. Overlap the beginning of the piping by 1 inch; then cut away any excess. Remove 1 inch of stitching from the end of the piping, push back the excess fabric and trim away only the cord so that the beginning and end of the cord are flush (Fig. 25). Now straighten out the excess fabric and finger-press the raw edge ½ inch to the wrong side (inside) by running your finger over the fold a few times. Slip the beginning of the piping inside the end so that the excess fabric covers all raw edges (Fig. 26); pin in place. Stitch the piping to the project all around.

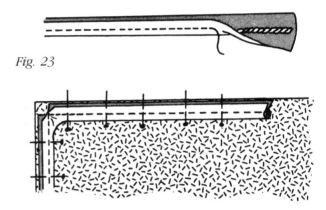

Fig. 23

Fig. 24

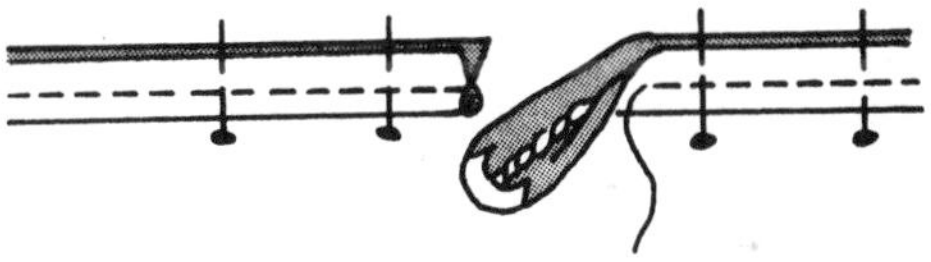

Fig. 25

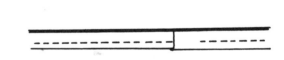

Fig. 26

EMBROIDERY

Hand embroidery can add a very special touch to a patchwork project. Often a few simple lines of embroidery can make a design come to life. Use any standard 6-strand cotton embroidery floss.

If the embroidery lines are given on a design, transfer the lines to the right side of your fabric using a hard lead pencil and graphite paper; or you can draw the design freehand on the fabric with a pencil.

Stretch the area to be embroidered in an embroidery hoop to hold the fabric taut; reposition the hoop as necessary while you are working. If the fabric sags in the hoop, pull it taut again. Embroider the design following the individual directions and stitch details (Fig. 27).

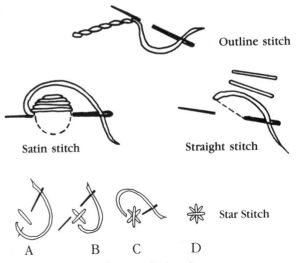

Outline stitch

Satin stitch   Straight stitch

A   B   C   D   Star Stitch

Fig. 27a   Embroidery stitch details

13

Each time you begin embroidering, leave extra floss dangling on the back of the fabric and embroider over it as you work to secure it, holding the floss flat against the fabric with your free hand. Do not make knots. To end a strand or begin a new one, weave the floss under the stitches on the back. From time to time, allow the needle and floss to hang straight down to unwind; this will prevent the floss from kinking or twisting while you embroider.

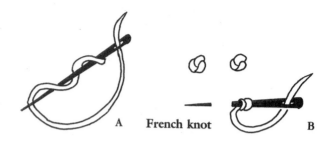

Fig. 27b   Embroidery stitch details, continued

HOW TO MITRE CORNERS

Fold the raw edges of adjacent border or binding strips back on themselves to form a 45° angle (Fig. 28.) Press. Pin and sew the edges together, matching the creases formed by the pressing. Check the right side to make sure that the corner is perfect, with no puckers. If there are puckers, you can usually correct them by removing one of the stitches. If the corner is perfect (Fig. 29), trim away the excess fabric, leaving a ¼-inch seam allowance. Press carefully.

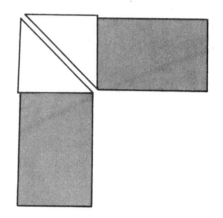

Fig. 28

LOOPS & TIES

Many of the projects in this book are meant to be hung or attached to something in some way. Loops and ties are made quickly and easily in a fabric that matches the binding.

Cut your chosen fabric to the size indicated for your project. Press the strip in half lengthwise, wrong sides together. Open the strip and press each of the long raw edges exactly to the pressed central fold, again with the wrong sides together. Fold and press each of the short ends ¼ inch to the wrong side; then press the strip in half again, sandwiching all raw edges inside; topstitch the folded edges together. Attach the loops or ties to the project following the individual instructions.

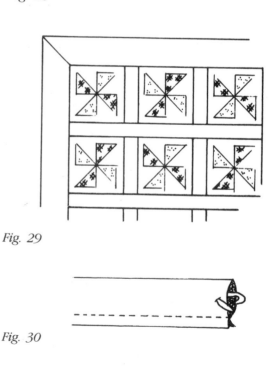

Fig. 29

USING A TUBE TURNER

A tube turner can be used to turn a loop, tie or strap inside out. There are 2 types of tube turners. The standard American style has a hook with a catch at the end as illustrated in Figs. 30 and 31; the British version has an eye at the end.

Stitch a strip of fabric together lengthwise with wrong sides facing, forming a tube. Insert the tube turner into the tube, gathering the strip onto the tube turner as necessary. Hook the end of the tube turner through the edge of the fabric, and work the

Fig. 30

Fig. 31

catch so that it holds the fabric securely in the hook (Fig. 30); or sew the eye of the tube turner to the edge of the fabric. Ease the fabric back over the tube turner, working it along section by section. Pull until the strip turns right side out (Fig. 31).

MAKING A BUTTONHOLE

Buttonholes made on the sewing machine are very quick and easy to do. First, lightly mark the position of the buttonhole on the fabric using a pencil. Attach a buttonhole foot to your sewing machine and set the machine as instructed in your manual. Work the buttonhole as directed in the manual. The usual method is to work a line of close zigzag satin stitches the entire length of the buttonhole (Fig. 32a). Zigzag back and forth at the bottom to secure the end; then satin-stitch back to the beginning; work more zigzag stitches at the beginning to secure that end (Fig. 32b). Finally, work a few stitches along the side of the buttonhole to secure

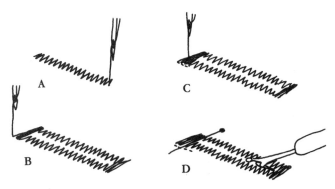

Fig. 32

the threads (Fig. 32c). Remove the fabric from the sewing machine. Using a seam ripper or a small pair of sharp scissors, carefully slit the buttonhole, placing a pin at the end of the buttonhole to prevent yourself from cutting too far (Fig. 32d).

If you do not have a sewing machine, or if you have a machine that does not do buttonholes, you can stitch the buttonhole by hand or substitute Velcro, snap fasteners or a hook and eye.

Batting

Batting (known as "wadding" in Great Britain), the central core of a quilted project, is available in polyester, cotton, and wool. For washability and ease in handling, select a polyester batting; it can be purchased in many sizes and weights. It is best to use a thin batting for small projects to keep the puffiness in scale with the size of the finished design. A thicker batting can be used for larger projects, such as blankets and wall hangings or for designs that are quilted and then stuffed, such as pillows.

Cotton and wool battings are a bit more difficult to handle, but quilters who prefer pure natural fibres strongly recommend them. Projects made with cotton or wool battings must be quilted at 1½-inch intervals to prevent lumps from forming when the project is washed. It is best to dry-clean projects made with cotton or wool batting, however.

Assembling a Project for Quilting

A quilt is actually like a sandwich, with the batting as the filling and the top and back as the bread. To make the sandwich, you'll need a large flat surface, such as a worktable or the floor.

Iron the back very well; tape it to the work surface, wrong side up, with the grain straight and all corners making 90° angles. Carefully place the batting over the middle of the back. If you must piece the batting, butt the edges and baste them together with large cross stitches.

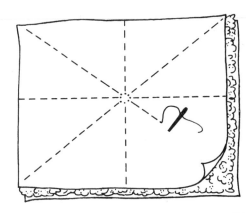

Fig. 33

Press the pieced top carefully—this will be the last time it will be ironed, so make the pressing a good one. Trim away any uneven seams on the back, and any threads or ravelled edges. When you are satisfied, set the top, right side up, over the batting, matching the outside edges.

Baste the 3 layers together quite thoroughly: First baste diagonally from the middle to each corner, then crosswise and lengthwise (Fig. 33). If you are using a quilting frame, put the quilt into the frame. If quilting with a hoop, add some additional basting (concentric squares) for extra safety.

You are now ready to quilt.

How to Quilt

You'll need a quilting or "between" needle, size 7 through 10 (10 is smallest); an 8 needle is a good size for most quilters. A thimble for the middle finger of your sewing hand is essential as is strong, mercerized 100-percent cotton quilting thread. Some quilters like to use a second thimble on the index finger of the hand under the quilt; this is optional.

To begin, cut an 18-inch length of quilting thread; thread your needle and knot the end of the thread. Run the needle and thread through the pieced top and some of the batting, pulling the knot beneath the surface of the quilt top (it usually makes a satisfying "popping" sound) and burying it in the batting (Fig. 34).

The quilting stitch is basically a running stitch. Hold the index finger of your left hand (for right-handed quilters) or right hand (for left-handed quilters) beneath the project just below the spot where you wish to make your stitches. Try to achieve a smooth rhythm, rocking your needle from the surface to the back, and then returning it again to the surface. Fig. 35 shows how to use the thimble to help push the needle through the fabric; the illustration also shows how the finger beneath pushes against the project to compress the batting, making it easier to take several stitches at a time. Aim to take 3 to 4 stitches at a time. Fig. 36 is a cross-section diagram showing how the quilting stitches should look when done correctly.

Don't panic if your stitches look larger than you think they should—an *even line* of stitches is the important thing, not the size of the stitches. The more you quilt, the smaller your stitches will become, but in the beginning, concentrate on making

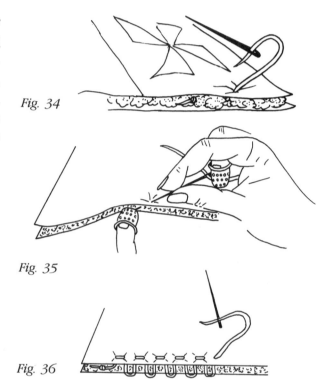

Fig. 34

Fig. 35

Fig. 36

the stitches approximately the same length on the top and on the back.

Suggestions for how to quilt each project are given at the end of each set of piecing instructions. For more quilting ideas, see the finished projects shown in the color section.

If you are using a hoop, baste strips of fabric, 6 to 12 inches wide, to the edges of the project so that it can be held in the hoop when you are quilting the outer edges.

In addition to the traditional type of quilting just described, 3 other methods are often used to quilt: machine quilting, the tufting stitch, and the quilt-as-you-go method. Follow the instructions below for each method.

16

MACHINE QUILTING

Insert a size-14 needle in your machine, loosen the thread tension slightly, and set the stitch length for 12 stitches per inch. Use a zigzag foot or attach a quilting foot if you have one. Spread the layers of your well-basted project under the machine foot with your hands to imitate the tension of a quilting frame. Stitch slowly. Always machine-quilt in the same direction across a project to prevent the layers from shifting. To prevent the top layer from easing ahead of the needle when sewing a long line, pin the 3 layers together directly over each line to be quilted.

Each time you begin and end a line of stitching, the thread ends must be finished off, which can be very time-consuming. For speedier machine quilting, adapt your designs so as to quilt in a continuous line, thus avoiding finishing off the threads too many times. To end a line of machine quilting, turn the project to the wrong side, and pull the thread end, drawing up the thread from the right side. Pull through gently. Knot the threads. Insert both threads into a needle and run them through the back and batting, bringing the needle out at least 1 inch away. Pull gently and clip away excess thread close to the fabric so that the ends will pop back into the batting out of sight.

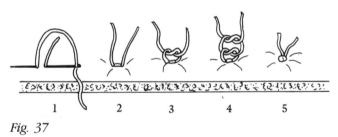

Fig. 37

TUFTING STITCH

The tufting stitch can be used on the right or wrong side of a project, depending upon whether or not you wish the knot to show. Following Fig. 37 and using a length of quilting thread, make a backstitch through all 3 layers of the project (1); the ends should be even (2). Tie the ends in a simple knot (3); tie another knot over the first (4). Pull tight and trim the ends close to the knot (5).

QUILT-AS-YOU-GO METHOD

Use the quilt-as-you-go technique for simple patchwork designs; piecing and quilting are done at the same time using a sewing machine. This method considerably shortens the time needed to make a project because when the sewing is done, the project is finished (except for the binding).

Follow the requirements for the project you are making to cut the back and batting pieces; the batting should be ¼ inch smaller than the back all around. Place the batting on the middle of the wrong side of the back; baste in place diagonally or horizontally and vertically so that the threads will cross in the exact middle of the block; these lines may serve as guidelines for placement of the patchwork. Place the basted piece, batting side up, on a flat surface. Position the first patchwork piece, right side up, on the batting and baste in place all around

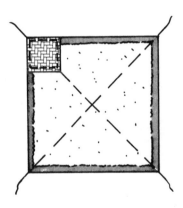

Fig. 38

(Fig. 38). Pin the second piece over the first with right sides together and raw edges even. Stitch together ¼ inch from the edge, making sure that all the layers feed smoothly under the presser foot of the sewing machine (Fig. 39). Remove the pins and

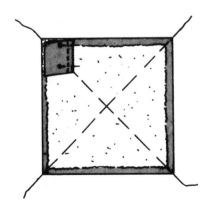

Fig. 39

fold the second piece to the right side; finger-press by running your finger over the seam a few times (Fig. 40). (Do not be tempted to use an iron for pressing or you may be faced with melted batting!) Continue adding pieces, as directed, until the entire base is covered, finger-pressing after each new piece is added. Complete the project, following the individual instructions.

Another quilt-as-you-go technique is to quilt individual patchwork blocks, then assemble them into a quilt or other project. Construct a patchwork block normally; then assemble the block with batting and a back, basting the layers together thoroughly. Quilt the single block by hand or machine. In this way, if you are quilting by hand, you can make a large quilt without having to carry the full weight of it around with you. You can quilt your project one block at a time; when it is finally joined together, it is completely finished! However, this presents its own special problems, particularly if you are planning to join the quilt blocks with sashing. The instructions that follow will guide you through this process.

QUILT-AS-YOU-GO: JOINING BLOCKS

Joining blocks with sashing in the quilt-as-you-go method is easy. When you cut out the sashing, cut double the number of pieces that are required: one in the fabric you plan to use on the quilt top (Fabric A), and one in the fabric that you are using to back the blocks (Fabric B). Baste a strip of batting to the wrong side of each A sashing strip (Fig. 41). Pin both the A and B sashing strips to the same edge of one quilted block: the right side of the B strip should face the back of the block and the right side of the padded A strip should face the front of the block. Stitch together (Fig. 42). Open out the padded strip only. Stitch a second block to the opposite long edge of the padded strip with right sides facing (Fig. 43). Fold the long raw edge of the B strip ¼ inch to the wrong side; smooth over the padded strip and pin so that the folded edge covers the stitching line. Slipstitch in place securely with matching thread (Fig. 44). Continue joining the blocks in this way, forming as many rows of blocks and sashing as are required. Join the rows of blocks and sashing with long padded sashing in the same manner. Bind the edges with a separate binding to complete your quilt.

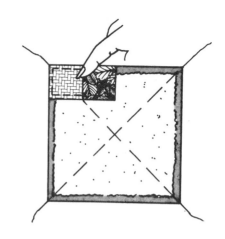

Fig. 40

Fig. 41

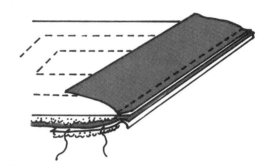

Fig. 42

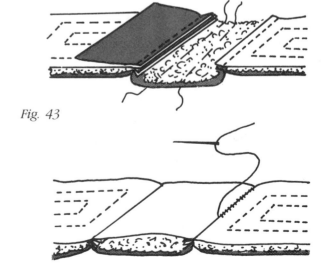

Fig. 43

Fig. 44

OUTLINE QUILTING

Work one row of quilting around the edge of a piece, either in the seam (called quilting "in-the-ditch") or just next to the seam as shown in the illustration (Fig. 45).

ECHO QUILTING

Work parallel lines of quilting to emphasize a portion of a design (Fig. 46). Lines can be ¼ to ½ inch apart, depending upon the size of the project. This is called "echo quilting" because the lines of stitching parallel or "echo" the shape of the piece you wish to accentuate.

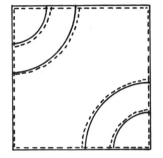
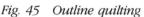
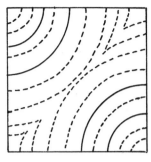

Fig. 45   Outline quilting   *Fig. 46   Echo quilting*

Binding a Project

When the quilting is finished, remove your basting stitches. You are now ready for the final step—the binding. The binding is the finishing touch to your project and should be used to enhance the overall design; give it careful consideration. All project requirements include the measurements for a separate binding, although many of the projects can be finished with self-binding or fold-finishing (see below). Usually, the binding is cut on the straight grain of the fabric, but there are times when the binding must be cut on the bias. While I usually do not recommend using a purchased binding, for a small project with curved edges, such as an ornament or Christmas stocking, it would be far easier—and much quicker!—to use double-fold bias tape.

SEPARATE BINDING

A separate binding takes a bit more time to prepare than a self-binding, but it gives you the freedom to choose any preferred color or print.

To prepare a separate binding, cut your chosen fabric to the length indicated with the requirements for your project. For a larger project, piecing will be necessary. Press the strip in half lengthwise, wrong sides together. Open the strip and press one long raw edge exactly to the pressed central fold, again with the wrong sides together; this folded edge is later slip-stitched to the back of the project.

With right sides together and raw edges even, pin the unpressed edge of the binding to the right side of the project. If you are binding a project with corners such as a quilt or wall hanging, allow extra fabric at each corner for mitring. For most other projects that do not require mitring, about ¼ inch excess fabric should extend beyond each edge of the piece you are binding; this excess fabric is later folded under to conceal the raw edges.

Start your stitching at the edge and stitch to the opposite edge, making a ¼-inch seam. Wrap the pressed edge of the binding over the raw edges of the project to the back; slip-stitch invisibly in place, folding the excess fabric at each end under to conceal the raw edges. Complete each strip of binding in turn before adding the next one.

SELF-BINDING

Self-binding is a quick and easy way to finish a quilted project. This technique is not always recommended when the back is made from the same fabric as the border because of the finished effect: self-binding can make the edges of the project seem to fade away, particularly if the colors of the project are very strong.

If you decide to self-bind your project, mark and cut an extra inch all around the edge of the fabric for the back; this will add 2 inches to the length and width measurements. Arrange the batting and top carefully over the lining to leave the inch-wide border free around the edges.

After the quilting is done, you can bind the project. Finger-press the edges of the back ½ inch inward to the wrong side of the fabric to make a folded edge. Then wrap the back towards the pieced top, covering the edges of the batting and top. Pin the folded edge to the top (Fig. 47). Slip-stitch the folded edge of the back invisibly to the top. Mitre the corners or conceal the raw ends, as necessary. Remove all pins when finished.

FOLD-FINISHING

This type of "binding" should be done *before* the project has been quilted. Trim the raw edges of the back even with the top; then fold the raw edges of both the top and back ¼ inch towards each other to conceal the raw edges inside the project. Slip-stitch together invisibly and securely. To quilt, baste strips of muslin to the finished edge of the project so that it can be placed in a frame or hoop.

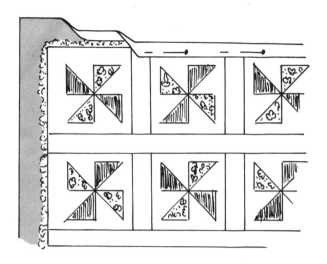

Fig. 47

Hanging a Patchwork Project

When a project is meant to be hung on a wall, measurements are always given for a sleeve. To attach a sleeve to a project, turn all raw edges ¼ inch to the wrong side; repeat the folding and topstitch in place so that all raw edges are hidden. Press. Pin the sleeve flat across the top of the project on the back, centering it between the sides. Slipstitch each long edge of the sleeve securely to the project back; do not allow your stitches to go through to the right side. Insert a rod through the sleeve for hanging.

Your Signature

Your project will have greater personal and historic value if it is signed and dated. Embroider your name and the date on the front or back with embroidery floss or sign your name and date on the back with indelible ink.

Block Designs
10-INCHES SQUARE

Budding Rose

Challenging
Pieces per block: 12

A	1 dark	G	1 light
B	1 bright	H	1 white, 1
C	1 bright		white reversed
D	1 medium	J	1 green, 1
E	1 medium		green reversed
F	1 light	K	1 green

Templates are on pages 23 and 24. Choose 4 varying shades of a single color for the flower, such as red, yellow, pink, or apricot. If you don't have 4 shades of a color, you can cut the A piece from a yellow fabric to simulate the flower center. Choose a pure white background to show the flower and leaves off to their best advantage. The block is challenging because insetting is required; see *How to Inset*. It is constructed from the corner square outward, similar to the Log Cabin design.

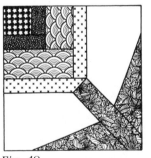 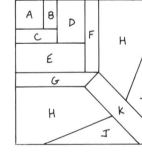

Fig. 48

Sew B to A. Sew C to A-B. Sew D to C-B. Sew E to C-D. Sew F to E-D. Sew G to E-F. Sew each H to a J. Sew the H-J pieces to opposite sides of K. Inset the flower into the H-K-H area to complete the design.

Outline-quilt each separate color strip on the flower; also outline-quilt the leaves and stem.

City Lights

Challenging
Pieces per block: 36

A	4 very dark, 4 medium reversed	C	8 pale
		D	4 light
		E	4 dark
B	4 dark	F	8 bright

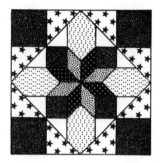 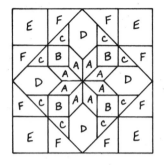

Fig. 49

Templates are on page 24. The 3-dimensional possibilities of this block make the effort of insetting worthwhile; review *How to Inset* before beginning. Study the assembly diagram carefully before you choose your own fabrics. Use a fabric with a large print for the F pieces to throw the central medallion into relief.

To begin, sew each medium A to a very dark A. Place the central star on a flat surface, and arrange the B, C and D pieces around it following the assembly diagram. Inset a D into A-A at the top, bottom and sides. Stitch a C to adjacent edges of each B. Inset B into the 4 corners of the star, continuing your stitching to sew the C and D pieces together. Sew an F to 2 adjacent edges of each E. Sew these 4 triangles to each edge of the central medallion to complete the design.

Outline-quilt each of the seams of this design.

Country House

Easy
Pieces per block: 18

A	1 striped	G	2 light, 2 bright
B	1 sky		
C	1 sky	H	3 striped
D	1 medium	J	1 striped
E	1 striped	K	1 medium
F	1 sky, 1 sky reversed	L	2 striped

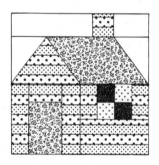 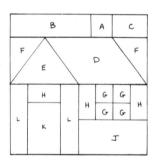

Fig. 50

Templates are on pages 25 and 26. Use a striped fabric to simulate the boards used to build a house; be sure to match the stripes carefully when cutting out the pieces.

For the chimney strip, sew B and C to opposite sides of A. To make the roof, sew E to D; then sew an F to each side edge. Sew the roof to the chimney strip for the top half of the block.

Sew the 4 G's together, alternating colors as shown in the diagram. Sew an H to each side. Sew H-G-G-H to J. Sew the remaining H to K; sew an L to each side. Sew L to H-J following the diagram.

To assemble the block, sew the 2 halves together.

Outline-quilt the edge of the house, the roof, the door and each window.

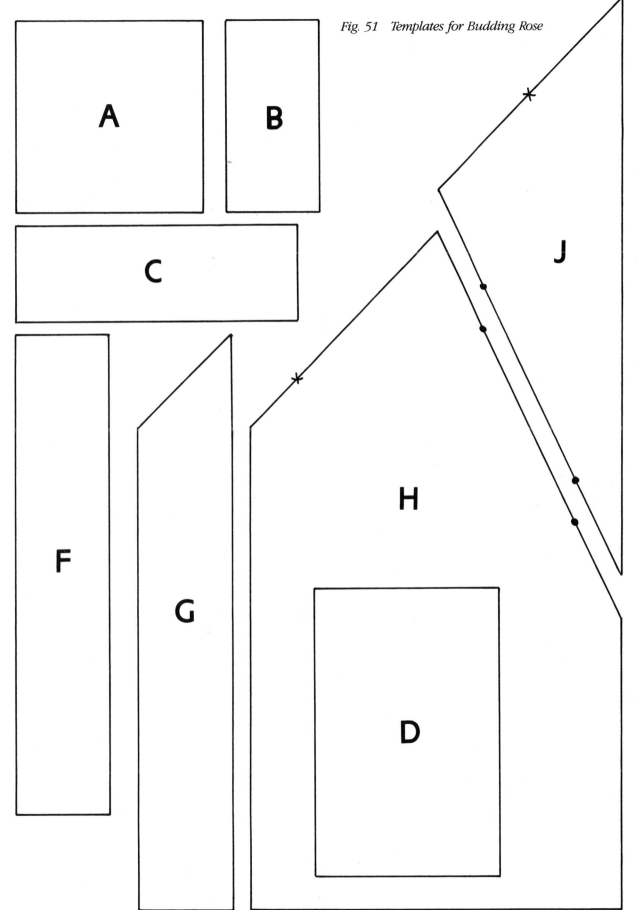

Fig. 51 Templates for Budding Rose

23

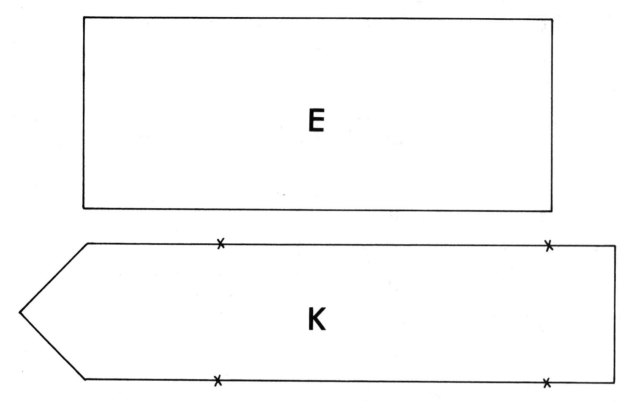

Fig. 52   Templates for Budding Rose, continued

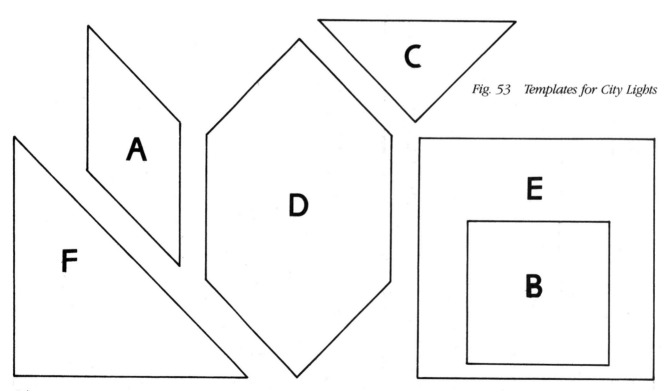

Fig. 53   Templates for City Lights

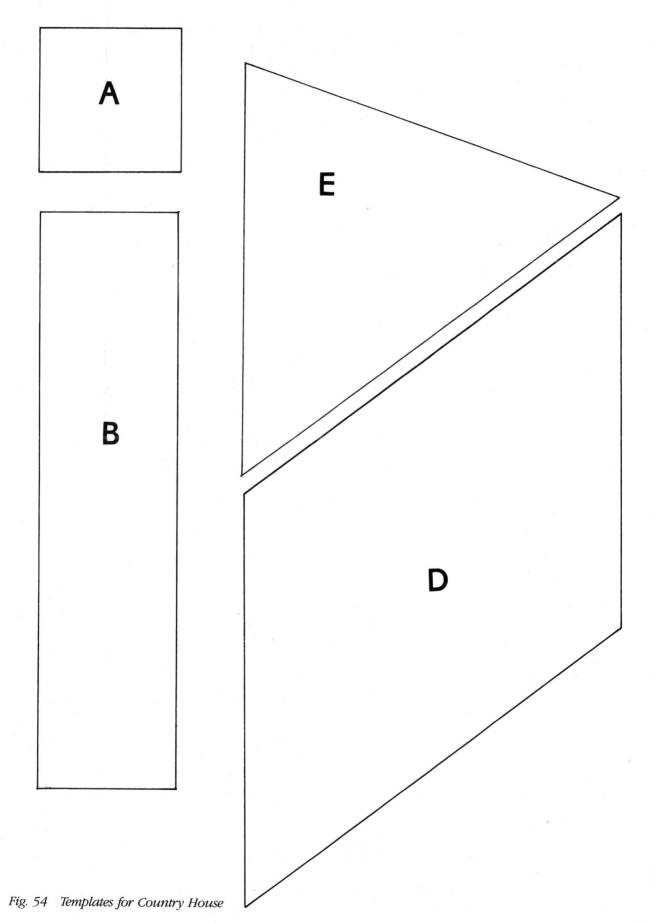

Fig. 54   Templates for Country House

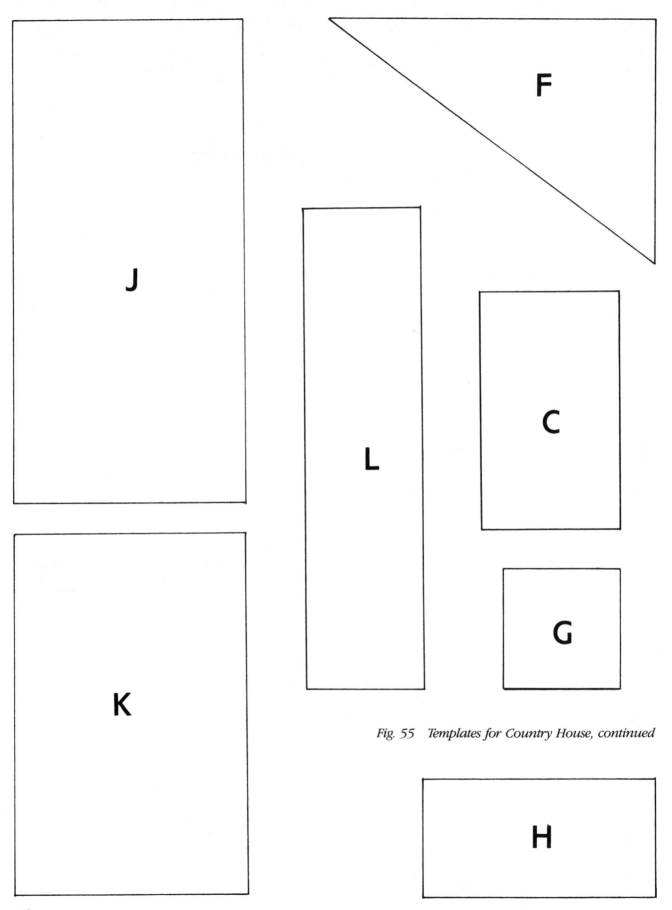

Fig. 55   Templates for Country House, continued

Double Pinwheel

Easy
Pieces per block: 12
A   4 light, 4 dark
B   4 bright

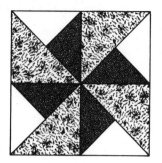 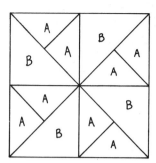

Fig. 56

Templates are on page 28. A good design for beginning quilters, this block is very fast and easy to complete. Take care when matching the seams in the middle.

The block is composed of 4 squares. To make each square, sew a light A to a dark A. Sew A-A to B. Arrange the squares as shown in the assembly diagram; sew 2 pairs of squares together to make each half. Sew the halves together to complete the design.

Outline-quilt the bright and dark pieces.

Feathery Star

Moderate
Pieces per block: 41

A   1 bright
B   8 light
C   24 bright
D   4 light
E   4 light

 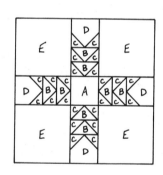

Fig. 57

Templates are on page 28. If you use a rotary cutter and chain-piece the B-C pieces, you can finish this block in much less time than you'd think. It isn't a difficult design, but its success depends upon careful piecing and matching of seams. The block is assembled in 3 horizontal rows.

First, assemble the 4 "feathery" arms of the star. Sew a C to adjacent edges of each B and D as shown. Stitch 4 pairs of C-B-C rectangles together; then sew a C-D-C to each B to complete each "arm." Arrange the pieces on a flat surface following the assembly diagram. Sew the C-C edge of 2 arms to each side of A. Sew an E to each side of the remaining 2 arms. Sew the rectangles just made to each side of the central A strip to complete the design.

Outline-quilt each of the bright A and C pieces.

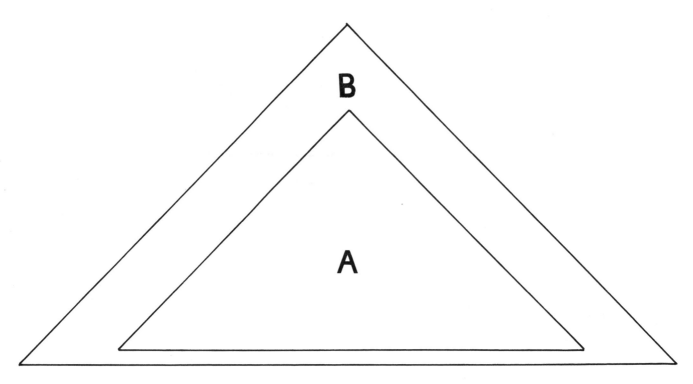

Fig. 58   Templates for Double Pinwheel

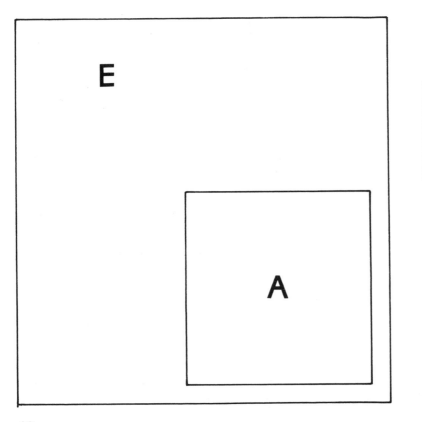

Fig. 59   Templates for Feathery Star

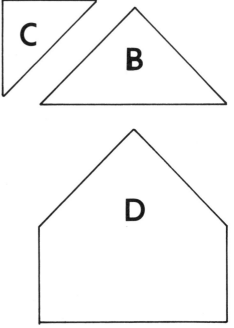

Flock of Geese

Easy
Pieces per block: 20
A   8 light, 8 dark
B   2 light, 2 dark

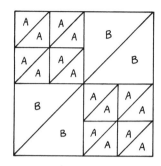
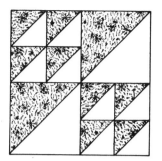

Fig. 60

Templates are on page 31. This traditional design is simple, yet effective. It consists of 4 pieced squares.

To begin, arrange the A and B pieces on a flat surface following the assembly diagrams. Next, sew each light A to a dark A, forming squares. Sew 2 pairs of squares together, forming rectangles; then sew the rectangles together forming the large A squares.

Sew each light B to a dark B, forming 2 squares. Sew each A square to a B square to form the upper and lower halves of the design. Press the seam allowances in opposite directions; then sew the upper and lower halves together to complete the design.

Quilt along each of the seam allowances. If desired, quilt an abstract flying bird design on each B piece as shown on the template.

Flower Basket

Easy
Pieces per block: 21
A   1 dark
B   2 dark
C   1 light, 1 light reversed
D   2 light, 4 assorted bright colors
E   2 light, 6 assorted bright colors
F   1 light, 1 light reversed

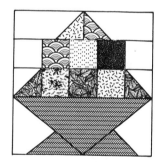
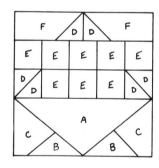

Fig. 61

Templates are on pages 31 and 32. Select a wild array of bright floral prints for the "flower" portion of this design. The block is assembled in 4 horizontal strips.

Begin by making the basket section. Sew each B to C, matching the dots. Sew B-C to opposite sides of A.

Arrange the D, E and F pieces on a flat surface above the basket section. Move the D and E pieces around until you have found the best mix of print and color; then stitch the pieces together in 3 horizontal rows. In the top row, stitch each F to a D; then stitch D-D together. In the middle row, stitch 5 E's together, with a light E at each end. In the bottom row, stitch 2 pairs of light and bright D's together;

stitch 3 bright E's together; then stitch D-D to each end of the E section, with the light D's outermost. Stitch these 3 strips together to complete the flower section.

Stitch the flower section to the basket section to complete the design.

Outline-quilt each bright D and E and the basket. Quilt a swirling floral-looking design across the "flowers" in the basket.

Hill House

Easy
Pieces per block: 18

A　1 sky
B　2 light
C　2 sky
D　1 dark
E　1 sky, 1 sky
　　reversed
F　1 light, 2
　　bright

G　1 bright
H　2 sky
J　1 medium
K　1 sky, 1 sky
　　reversed
L　1 sky

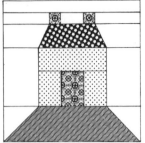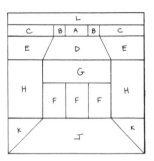

Fig. 62

Templates are on pages 32 and 33. Bold and simple, this block would be very effective if repeated in different color combinations to make up a single-design quilt or wall hanging.

For the chimney strip, sew B to each side of A; sew C to each B. For the roof, sew E to each edge of D. To assemble the house, sew a bright F to each side of the light F; sew the piece just made to G. Sew an H to each side of G-F. Make the hill by sewing K to each edge of J.

To assemble the block, sew L to the chimney strip. Sew the chimney strip to the roof; then sew the roof to the house. Sew the house on top of the hill to complete the design.

Outline-quilt the house, roof, chimneys and door. Quilt the hill with a series of crisscrossing diagonal lines. Quilt a swirling cloud pattern across the sky.

Home Sweet Home

Easy
Pieces per block: 20

A　1 sky
B　2 pale, 2 light,
　　2 sky
C　1 medium
D　1 sky, 1 sky
　　reversed

E　4 bright
F　2 bright
G　1 light
H　1 bright, 1 sky
J　1 dark

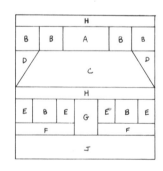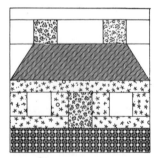

Fig. 63

Templates are on page 34. This solid, stable house design would make an effective central block in a wall hanging or quilt. It is joined in horizontal strips.

For the chimney strip, sew a light B to each side of A; then sew a sky B to each end. For the roof, sew a D to each edge of C. For the house, sew an E to each side of the pale B pieces; then sew an F to the long edges thus formed. Sew the rectangles just made to each side of G as shown in the diagram.

To assemble the block, sew the sky H piece to the chimney strip. Sew the chimney strip to the roof; then sew the roof to the bright H piece. Sew the bottom edge of the house to J; then sew the 2 halves together to complete the design.

Outline-quilt the edge of the house, door and windows. Quilt some swirling lines across the sky to simulate clouds; quilt J with parallel vertical lines to resemble grass.

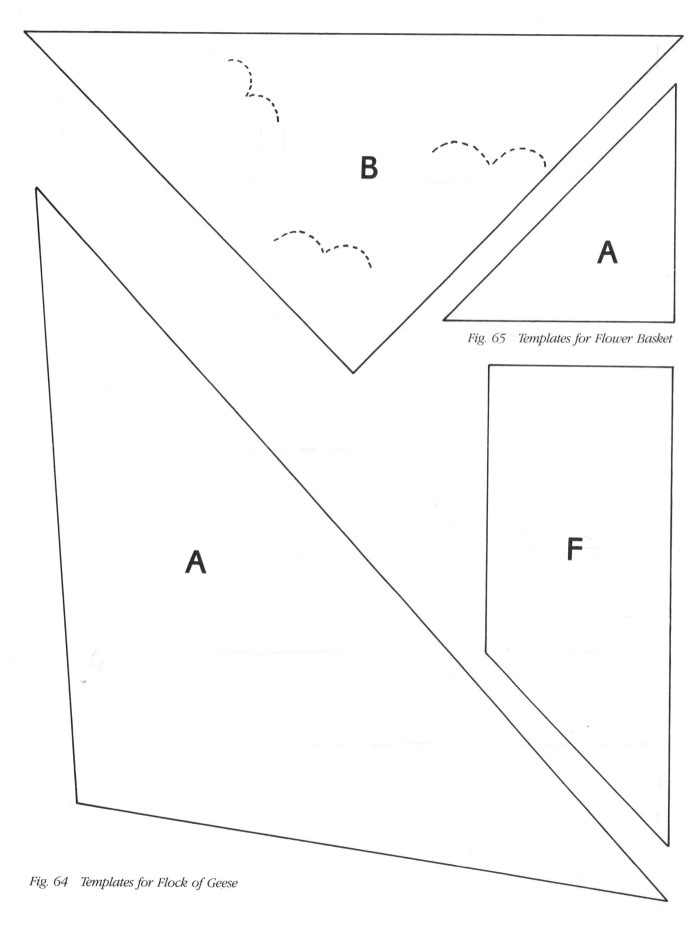

B

A

Fig. 65   Templates for Flower Basket

F

A

Fig. 64   Templates for Flock of Geese

31

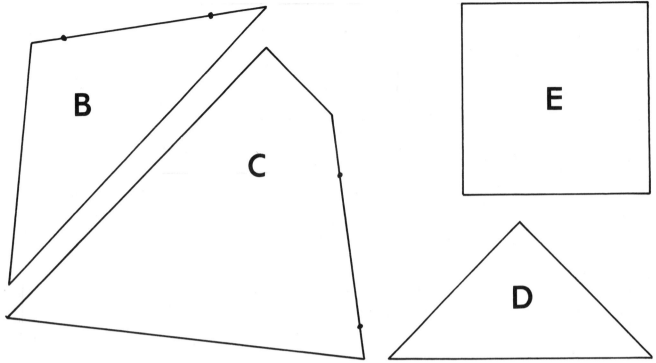

Fig. 66   Templates for Flower Basket, continued

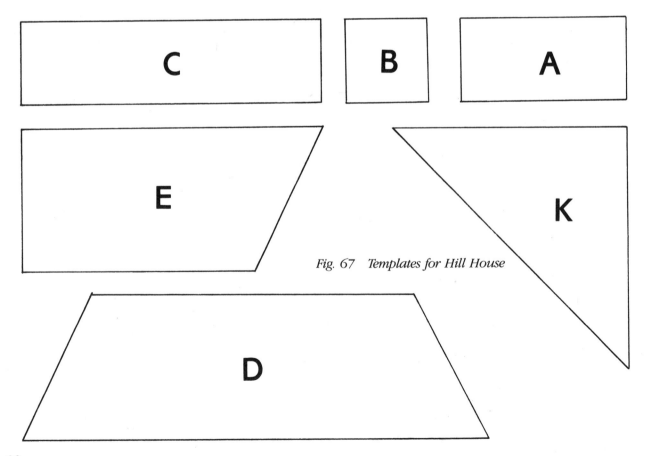

Fig. 67   Templates for Hill House

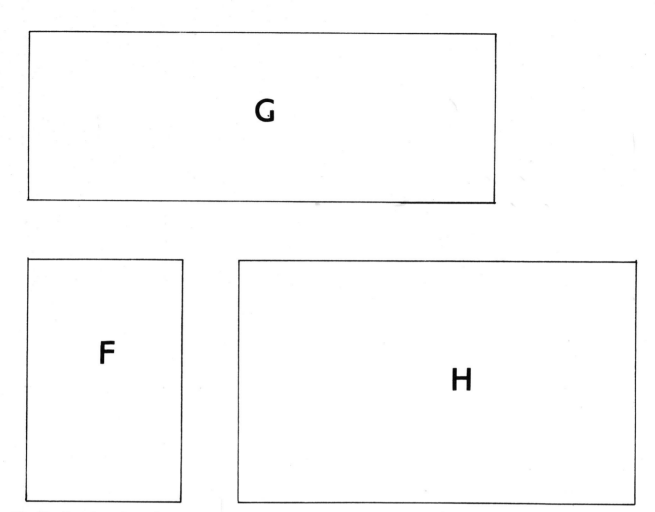

Fig. 68   *Templates for Hill House, continued*

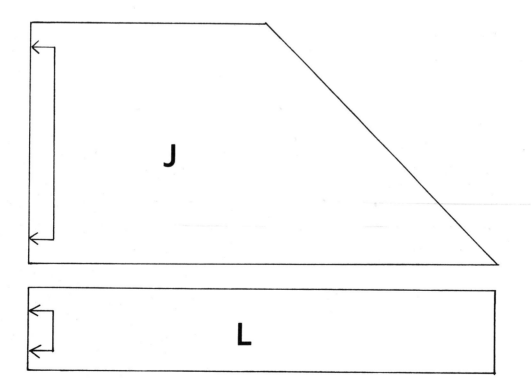

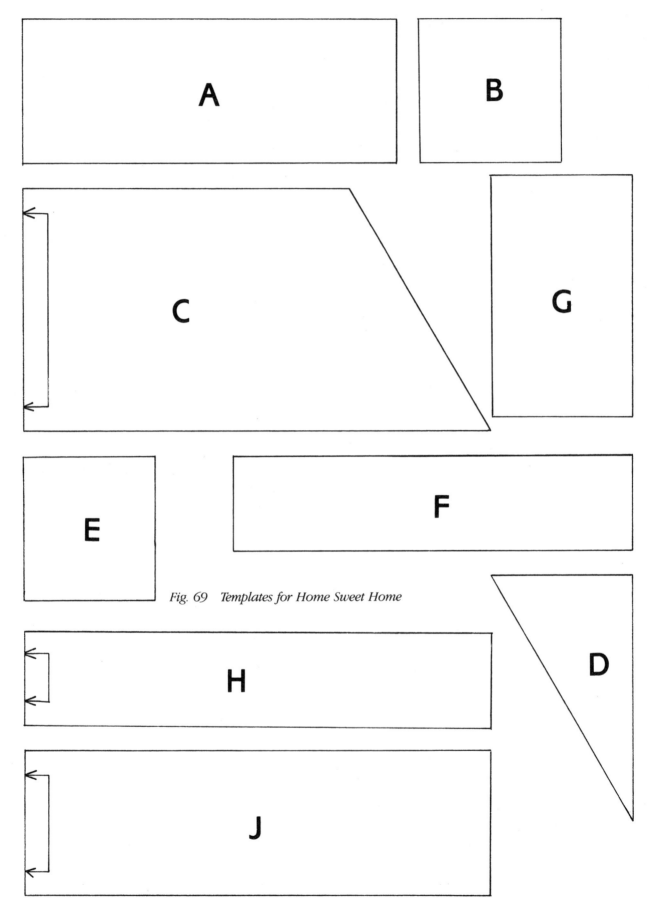

Fig. 69   Templates for Home Sweet Home

34

House in a Field

Moderate

Pieces per block: 32

A	1 bright	L	1 dark
B	1 sky	M	1 dark
C	1 dark	N	1 dark
D	1 bright	O	1 dark
E	1 sky	P	1 light
F	1 light	Q	1 dark
G	2 dark	R	1 sky
H	1 dark	S	1 medium
J	5 bright, 4 dark	T	1 medium, 1 sky
K	4 dark		

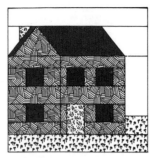

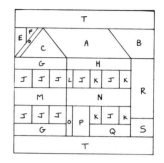

Fig. 70

Templates are on pages 36 and 37. Although there are many different pieces, this design is relatively easy to make. It is assembled in horizontal strips.

For the roof, sew B to A; then sew C to the opposite edge of A. Sew D to C. Sew E to F; then sew E-F to D.

For the house, sew G to H. Following the diagram, assemble the pieces for the top row of windows and sew together. Sew the window strip to G-H. Sew M to N; then sew to the lower edge of the window strip. Sew a dark J to each side of a bright J; sew a K to each side of the remaining bright J. Sew G to J-J-J; sew Q to K-J-K. Sew O to P; then sew J-G to O, and P to K-Q. Sew the rectangle just made to M-N. Sew R to S; then sew to the right edge of the house.

To assemble the block, sew sky T to the roof strip; sew the roof strip to the house. Sew the house to the medium T to complete the design.

Outline-quilt the house, roof, chimney, all the windows and the door.

Jitterbug

Moderate

Pieces per block: 23

A	1 bright	E	8 bright
B	2 dark	F	2 dark, 2 dark reversed
C	4 medium		
D	4 light		

Templates are on pages 37 and 38. Choose highly contrasting fabrics for the square so that it seems to float above the background pieces. Before beginning, arrange all the pieces on a flat surface, following the assembly diagram, for ease in construction.

First, construct the central square by sewing a B to opposite sides of A. Sew a C to opposite sides of the square just made. Sew a D to each end of the remaining C pieces; sew D-C-D to each remaining edge of the central square.

Next, construct each of the corner triangles. Sew

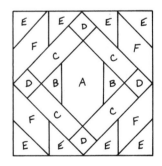

Fig. 71

an E to each F, matching the X's. Then sew an E to an adjacent edge of each F, matching the dots. (Dots are printed on 2 sides of each E piece, but you will only need match the dots along 1 edge per piece.) Finally, sew a corner triangle to each D-C-D edge to complete the design.

Outline-quilt the light, medium and dark pieces.

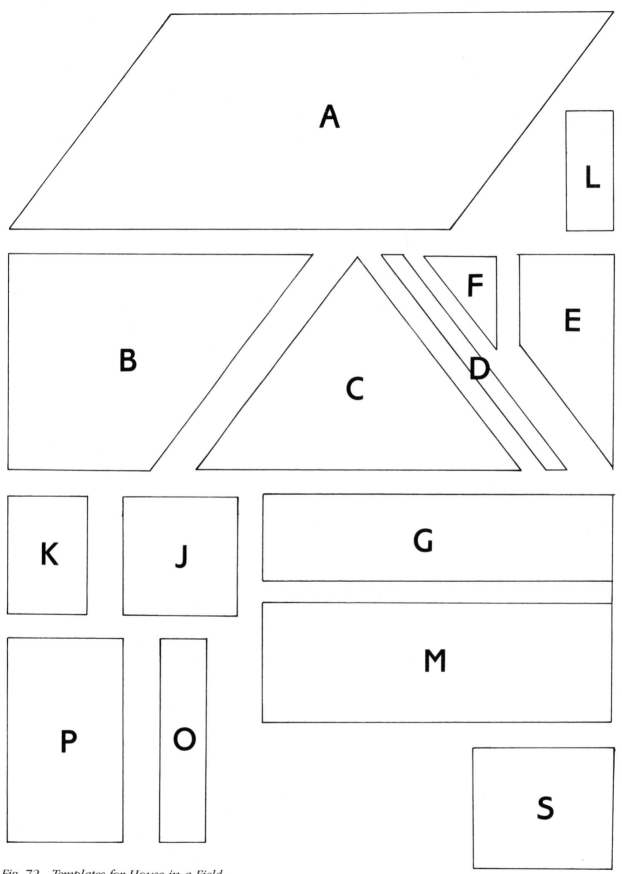

Fig. 72   *Templates for House in a Field*

36

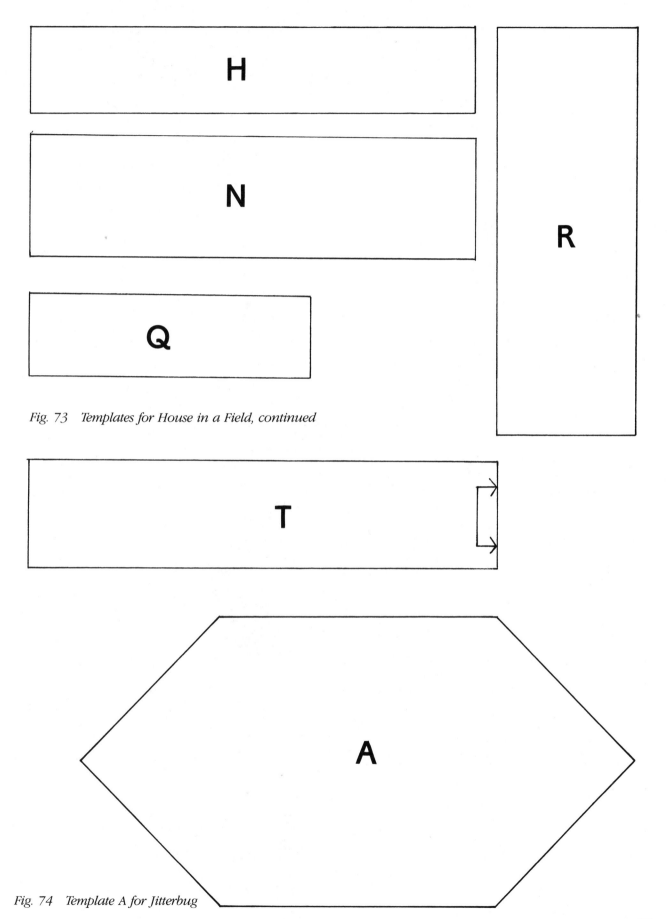

Fig. 73   Templates for House in a Field, continued

Fig. 74   Template A for Jitterbug

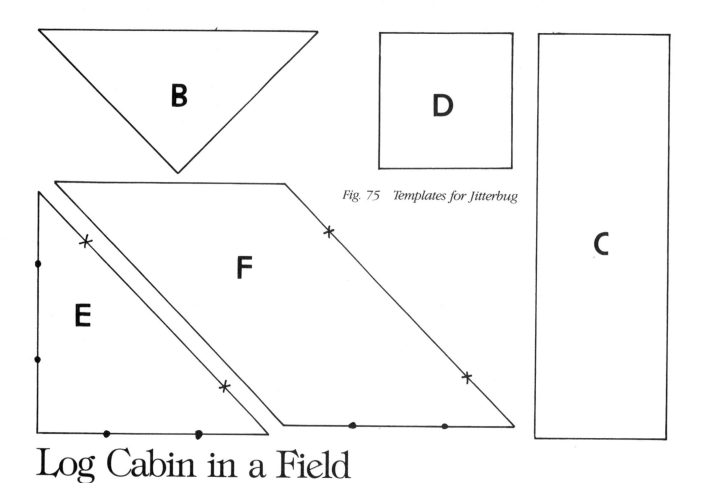

Fig. 75   Templates for Jitterbug

Log Cabin in a Field

Easy
Pieces per block: 21

A 1 dark
B 1 striped, 1
    striped
    reversed, 1 sky
    reversed
C 1 sky
D 1 sky
E 1 sky
F 1 bright
G 1 bright
H 1 medium, 1
    medium
    reversed
J 2 striped
K 1 sky
L 1 pale, 2
    striped
M 1 striped
N 1 light
O 1 grass
P 1 grass

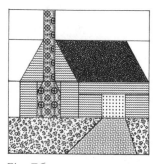
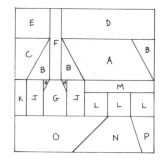

Fig. 76

Templates are on pages 39 and 40. Use a pretty striped fabric to simulate logs; be sure to match the stripes carefully when cutting out the pieces. The block is constructed in 2 halves.

For the upper half, sew sky B to the right edge of A; sew medium B to the opposite edge. Sew D to B-A-B. Sew C to the remaining B; then sew C to E. Sew the pieces just made to each side of F to complete the upper half.

For the lower half, sew H to each angled edge of G; sew J to each G-H side. Sew K to the left-hand J. Sew a medium L to each side of the pale L; sew M to the L strip. Sew M-L to J. Sew O and P to opposite sides of N; sew this strip to the bottom of the house to complete the lower half.

To assemble the block, sew the 2 halves together, matching seams carefully.

Outline-quilt the house, chimney, roof, door and path. Quilt horizontal lines across the house to simulate logs. Quilt lines across O and P to resemble grass.

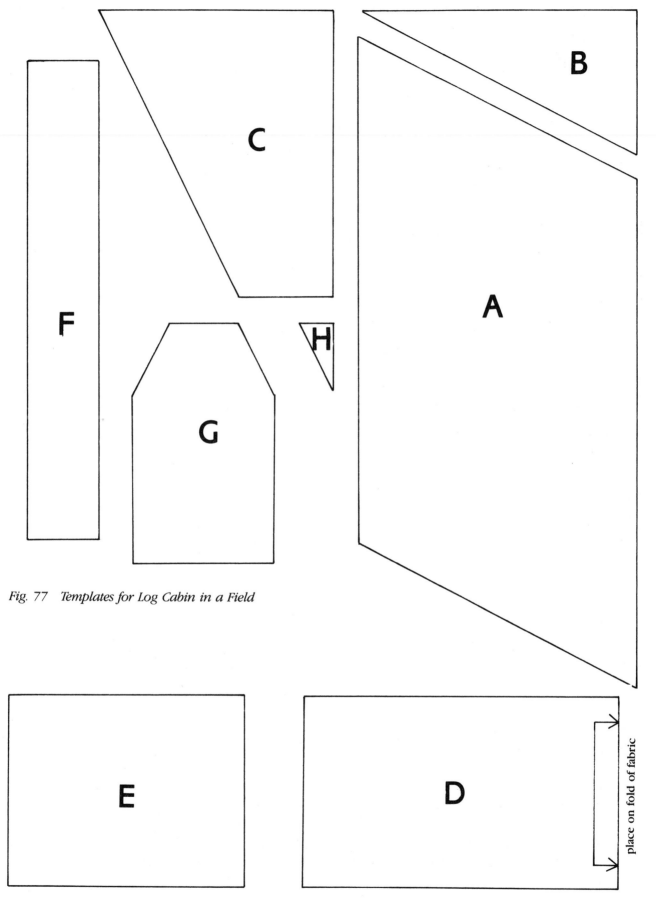

Fig. 77   Templates for Log Cabin in a Field

place on fold of fabric

39

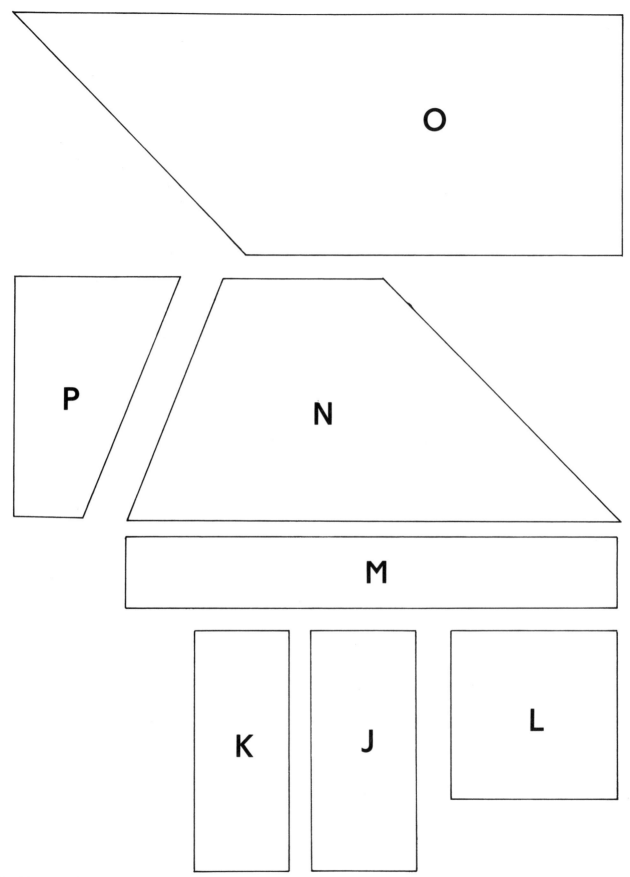

Fig. 78   Templates for Log Cabin in a Field, continued

40

Lucky Star

Easy
Pieces per block: 24

A   4 bright, 4
    dark
B   4 light

C   4 medium, 4
    medium
    reversed
D   4 medium

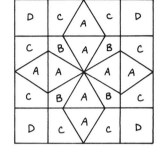

Fig. 79

With only a subtle change in color between the bright and dark A pieces, the star will appear to change intensity from the middle outward. Choose a relatively unobtrusive fabric for the medium pieces to make the star appear to stand out from the background. If you wish to add extra interest to the design, cut the D pieces from a light fabric.

Construct the central square first. Sew each dark A to a B matching the dots; then sew 2 pairs of A-B pieces together for each half of the square. Press the seam allowances in opposite directions. Stitch the halves together, matching seams carefully in the middle.

Stitch a C to each side of the bright A's, matching the dots. Sew a C-A-C rectangle to each side of the central square, matching the X's and the edges of the A seams carefully. Sew a D to each edge of the remaining C-A-C rectangles. Sew these strips to the top and bottom of the central section to complete the design.

Outline-quilt the star formed by the A pieces. To accentuate the star, add extra rows of echo quilting.

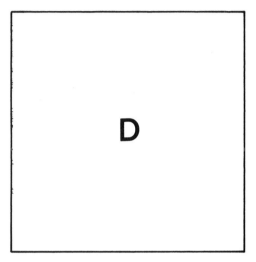

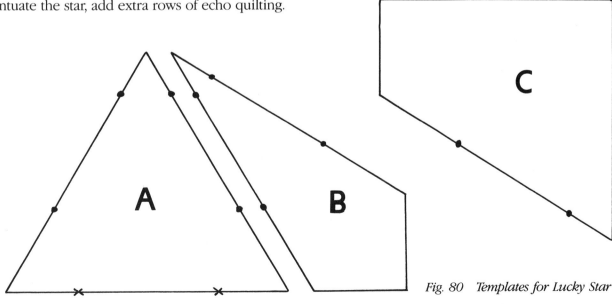

Fig. 80   Templates for Lucky Star

41

Maple Leaf

Easy
Pieces per block: 15

A 1 light, 3 dark   C 1 dark
B 4 light, 4 dark   D 2 light

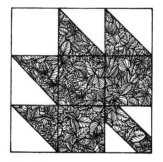
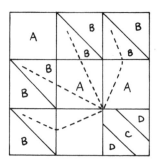

A traditional favorite, Maple Leaf can be made in many color combinations, but choose highly contrasting fabrics for the best effect. The block is assembled in 3 horizontal strips.

To begin, sew each light B to a dark B. Sew a D to opposite sides of C. Next, arrange the pieces in 3 horizontal rows as shown in the assembly diagrams. Sew the pieces together in rows; then sew the rows together, matching seams carefully to finish the design.

Fig. 81

Outline-quilt the leaf itself; then quilt "veins" on the leaf as shown in the assembly diagram.

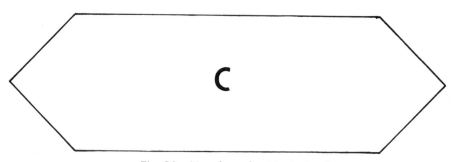

Fig. 82 Templates for Maple Leaf

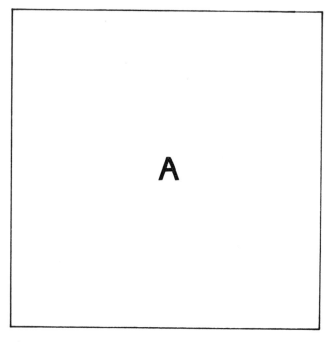

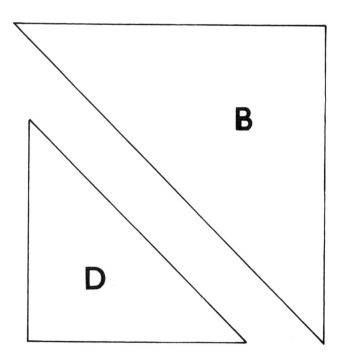

Regatta

Easy
Pieces per block: 8

A	1 dark	E	1 white
B	2 medium	F	1 sky
C	1 white	G	1 dark
D	1 sky		

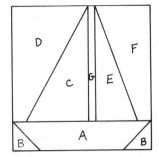

Fig. 83

Templates are on pages 44 and 45. Those with a nautical bent will be pleased to receive a gift featuring this design. Use highly contrasting colors for the sails, hull and sky.

To assemble the hull, sew a B to each side of A. To assemble the sails, sew D to C. Sew E to F; then sew C and E to opposite sides of G. Sew the sails to the hull to complete the design.

Outline-quilt the sails and hull. If desired, quilt a numeral on one of the sails. Quilt a swirling pattern across the sky to simulate clouds.

Schoolhouse

Moderate
Pieces per block: 24

A	1 light	G	1 dark
B	2 dark	H	3 light, 5 dark
C	2 light	J	1 dark
D	1 dark	K	1 dark
E	1 light, 1 light reversed	L	1 light, 2 dark
F	1 light	M	1 light

Fig. 84

Templates are on pages 46 and 47. Probably the most well known of the traditional "house" designs, Schoolhouse is a very popular choice when making a quilt or other project for small children. It is essential to match the B, F and M pieces quite carefully to achieve the best effect.

Begin with the chimney strip. Sew a B to opposite sides of A. Sew a C to each B. Next, construct the roof: Sew E and F to opposite sides of D. Sew G to F; then sew the remaining E to G. Sew the chimney and roof strips together to complete the top of the design.

Sew the H pieces together, alternating light and dark, as shown in the assembly diagram. Sew J and K to opposite sides of the 3 H's; sew a dark L to opposite sides of the 5 H's. Sew the light L to one dark L. Sew J-H-K and L-L-H-L to opposite sides of M, making sure that the light L is at the top.

Sew the top and bottom portions of the block together, matching seams carefully, to complete the design.

Outline-quilt the windows and all the light pieces.

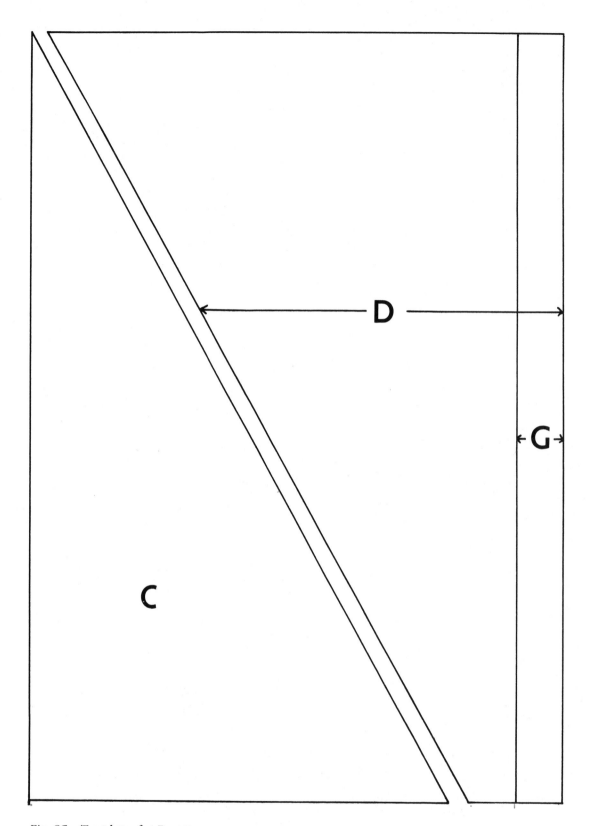

Fig. 85   Templates for Regatta

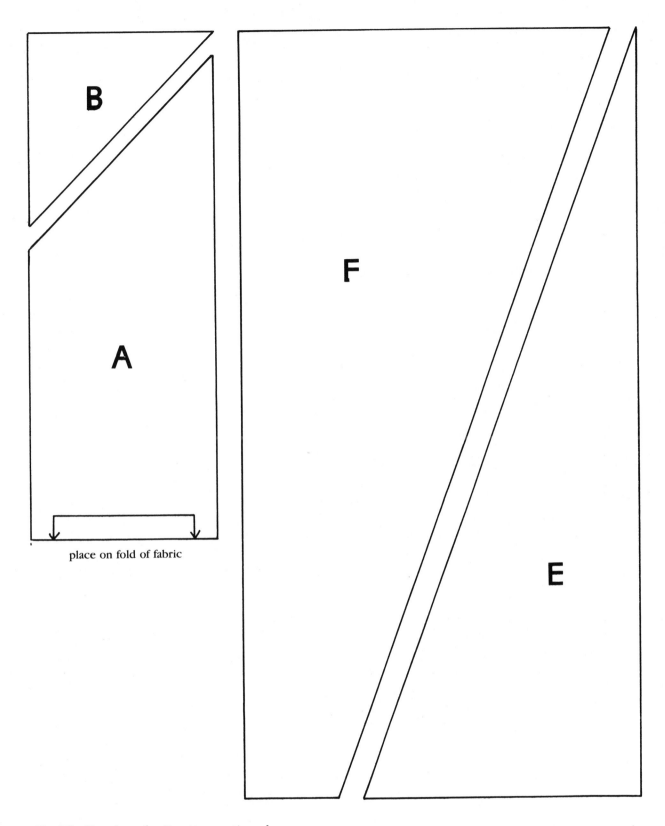

B

A

place on fold of fabric

F

E

Fig. 86   Templates for Regatta, continued

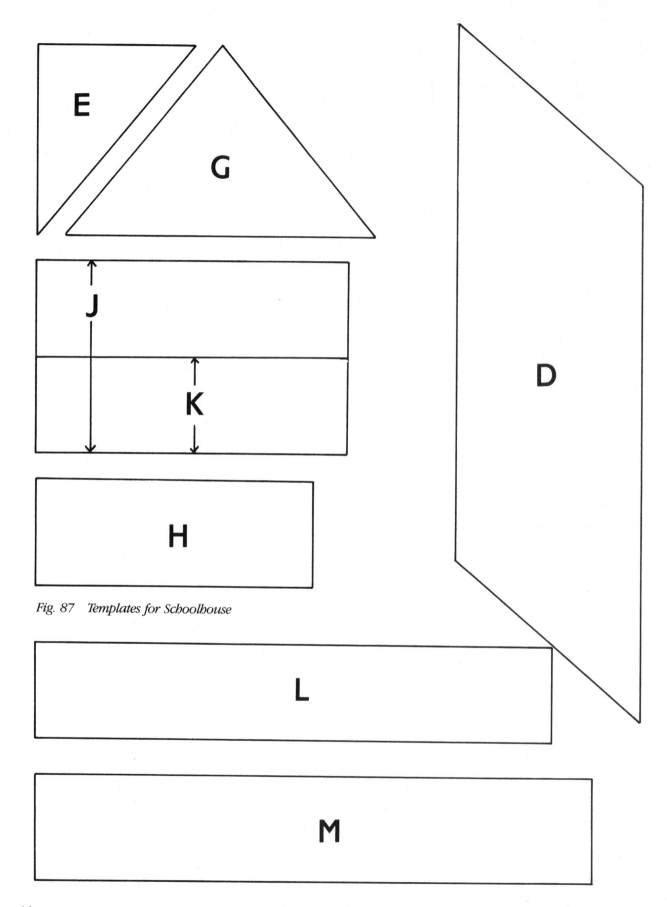

Fig. 87   Templates for Schoolhouse

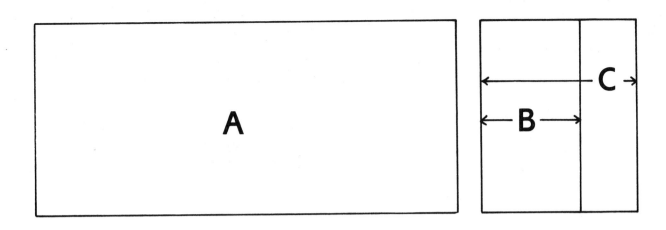

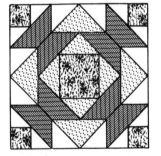

Fig. 88   Templates for Schoolhouse, continued

Small Baskets

Moderate
Pieces per block: 37

A	1 bright	E	8 light
B	4 medium	F	8 light
C	8 dark	G	4 bright
D	4 medium		

Templates are on pages 49 and 50. Select a very bright and flowery fabric for the A and G pieces to simulate baskets of lovely flowers. This block would create an interesting repeat pattern if you made several blocks and sewed them edge to edge. The stitching isn't difficult, but it takes a while to sew 37 little pieces together!

The block is assembled from the middle outward. Sew a B to each edge of A. Sew a C to each B-B edge. Sew a D to each C-C edge. Next, assemble each of the corner triangles. Sew an E to each angled edge

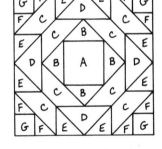

Fig. 89

of the remaining C's. Sew 2 F's to adjacent edges of each G. Sew F-F to the long edge of each C. Sew the triangles thus made to each D-C-D edge, matching the seams of the C pieces carefully.

Outline-quilt the A, C and G pieces.

Starlight

Easy
Pieces per block: 16

A 4 dark
B 4 light reversed
C 4 light reversed

D 4 dark reversed

I experimented with a striped effect on the assembly diagram, and it seems to work very well. Choose closely spaced stripes for a particularly dramatic result. The block is composed of 4 squares.

To construct each square, sew B and C to opposite sides of A. Sew D to each B-C edge. Sew 2 pairs of squares together for each half of the block. Sew halves together, matching seams carefully, to complete the design.

Outline-quilt the A and D pieces.

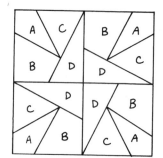

Fig. 90

Stripy Star

Challenging
Pieces per block: 44

A 4 light, 4 dark reversed
B 4 light, 4 dark reversed
C 4 light, 4 dark reversed

D 4 light, 4 dark reversed
E 4 light, 4 dark reversed
F 4 contrasting

Templates are on page 50. Use 5 different shades of light fabrics and 5 different shades of dark fabrics for pieces A through E. Use highly contrasting shades of light and dark for the best possible 3-dimensional effect. This block is challenging because of the difficulty in selecting just the right colors, and because insetting is required. Please review *How to Inset.*

Construct each light part of the star by sewing light A to light B to light C to light D to light E; press all seams towards the tip. Repeat for each of the dark parts of the star in the same manner, pressing all seams towards the base. Sew each light half of an arm to a dark one, matching all seams carefully.

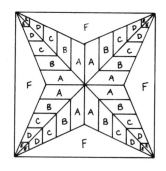

Fig. 91

Arrange the pieces on a flat surface as shown in the diagram. Sew the 2 upper arms together at the A edges; repeat for the 2 lower arms. Press the seam allowances in opposite directions. Stitch the upper and lower arms of the star together to complete the central part of the design. Inset the F pieces into the arms of the star to complete the block.

Outline-quilt each of the stripes.

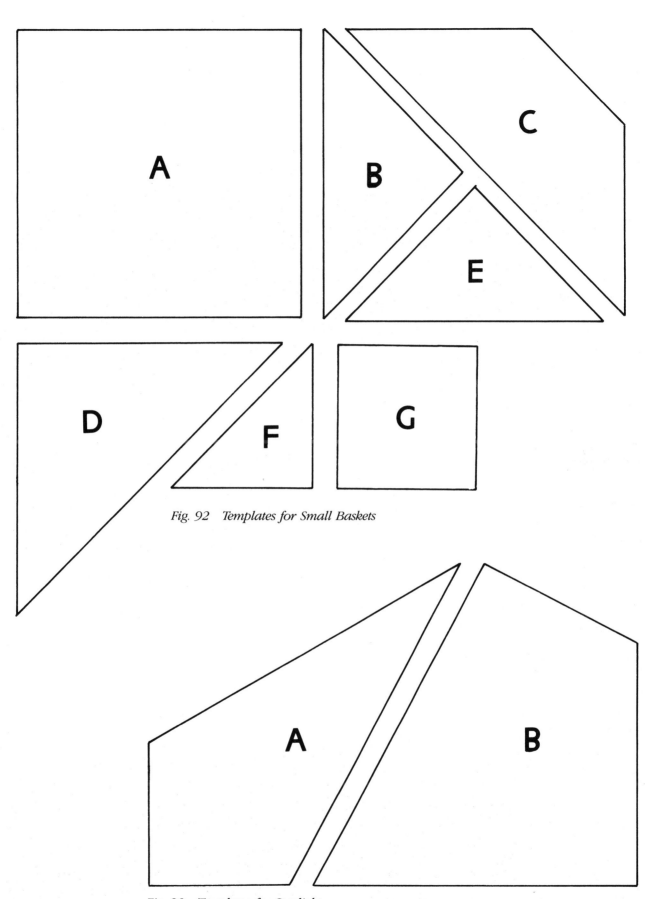

Fig. 92   Templates for Small Baskets

Fig. 93   Templates for Starlight

49

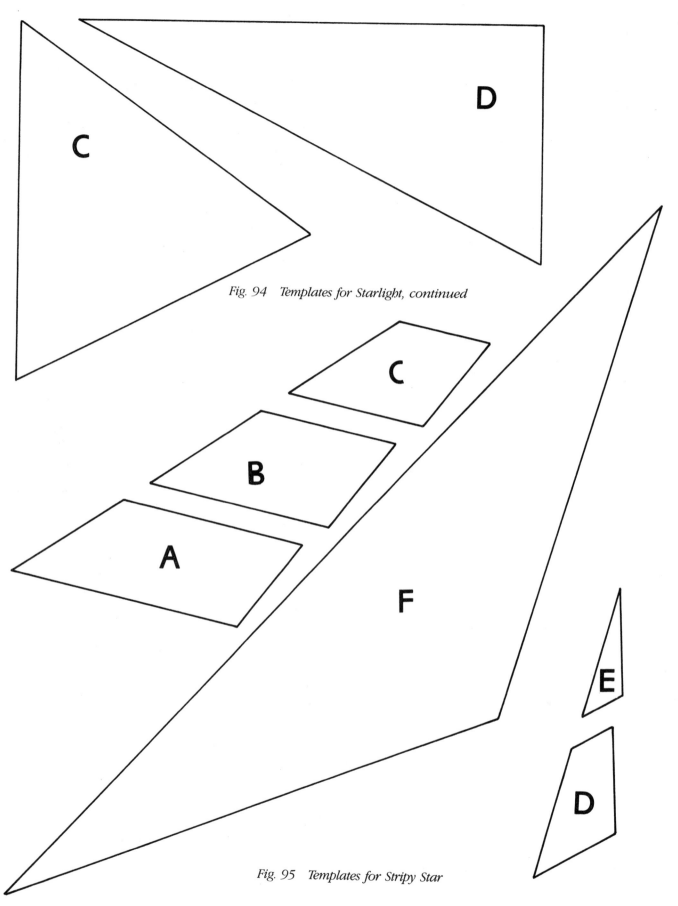

Fig. 94   Templates for Starlight, continued

Fig. 95   Templates for Stripy Star

Swing Music

Moderate
Pieces per block: 48
A   4 light
B   8 light, 16 medium
C   4 dark, 4 light reversed
D   4 medium
E   8 light

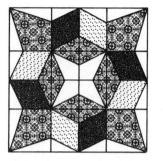

Fig. 96

Try different color combinations than the one shown here, because you can create many extraordinary effects with this multifaceted design. It is constructed in 4 horizontal rows; take care to match seams perfectly to keep the 3-dimensional effect.

To begin, sew a medium B to each long edge of A. Sew 1 light and 1 medium B to each long edge of each C. Sew an E to each long edge of each D. Following the assembly diagrams, arrange the pieced squares and rectangles in 4 horizontal rows, carefully positioning the light and dark C pieces as shown. Join the pieces making up each row together. Press the seams in opposite directions in each row; then sew the rows together, matching seams carefully.

Outline-quilt the central star; then quilt the inner and outer edges of the C and D pieces.

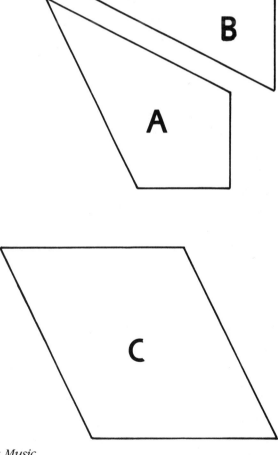

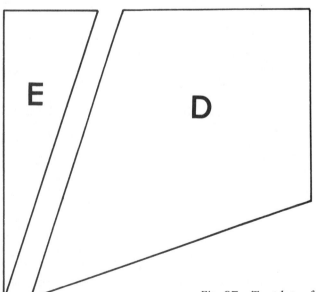

Fig. 97   Templates for Swing Music

Whirling Cross

Easy
Pieces per block: 16
A   8 light,
    4 medium,
    4 dark

A feeling of motion is achieved through the combination of these crooked-looking pieces. This would be an excellent design for a full-size quilt, with the blocks sewn edge to edge. You would then create a whole series of whirling crosses and the effect would be truly dramatic. The block is composed of 4 squares; be very careful to match the seams in the middle of each square.

Assemble all of your pieces on a flat surface following the diagram. Each square is composed of 2 halves. Sew a medium A to a light A and a dark A to a light A as shown in the assembly diagram. Sew the halves together to make each square. Sew the squares together with the dark A's in the middle to complete the design.

Outline-quilt the dark and medium pieces.

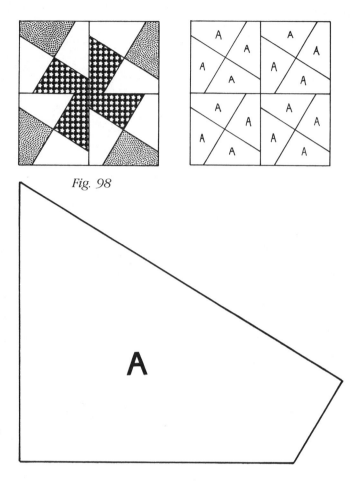

Fig. 98

Fig. 99   Template for Whirling Cross

Wildflower

Challenging
Pieces per block: 13

A   3 light,   D   1 dark, 1 dark
    3 bright   reversed
B   1 dark   E   1 light, 1 light
C   2 light   reversed

Templates are on page 52. Designed with an "Art Deco" feel, this geometric flower will enhance any project you choose to make. Review *How to Inset* before beginning.

To make the flower, sew each light A to a bright A. Sew a C to each long edge of B. Arrange these 4 squares on a flat surface as shown in the assembly diagram. Sew 2 pairs of squares together; press the seam allowances in opposite directions. Sew the stitched pairs together, matching seams carefully.

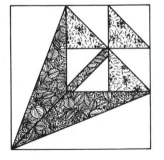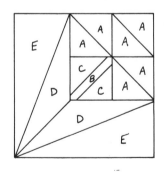

Fig. 100

For the leaves, sew each E to a D. Sew the D's together. Inset the flower into the angle formed by the 2 D's to complete the design.

Outline-quilt the flower, stem and leaves.

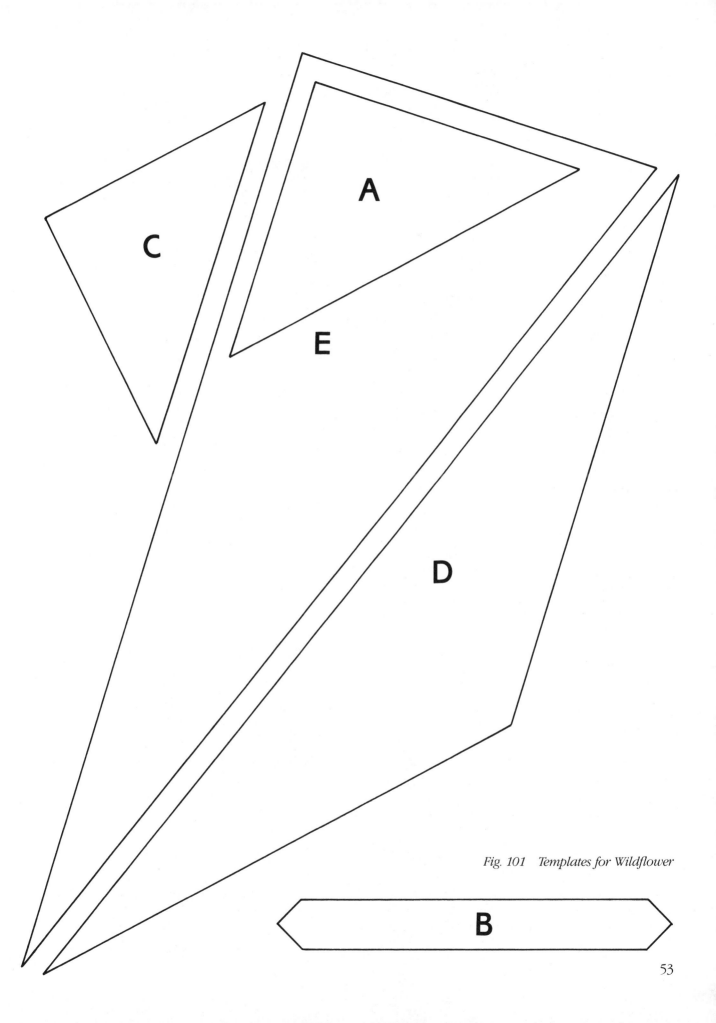

Fig. 101   Templates for Wildflower

Wishing Star

Moderate
Pieces per block: 20

A	2 bright, 2 medium	D	4 dark
B	4 bright	E	4 light
C	4 light		

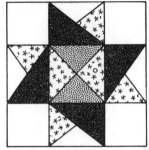
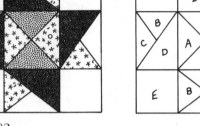

Fig. 102

Templates are on page 55. Make this block in the color scheme given above and you'll end up with what looks like 2 stars overlapping one another. However, you can achieve an entirely different effect if you make the central portion entirely in a striped fabric, as shown in the alternate assembly diagram; it would be fun to experiment with stripes this way.

The block is assembled in 3 horizontal rows. Assemble the pieces on a flat surface following the assembly diagram of your choice. Begin with the central square. Sew a bright A to each medium A, matching the X's; sew A-A to A-A matching the seams in the middle. Sew each B to C, matching the dots; sew B-C to D matching the dots and diamonds. Sew

a B-C-D rectangle to each side of the central A square. Sew an E to each side of the remaining B-C-D rectangles. Sew these 3 rows together, matching seams carefully.

Outline-quilt the bright and dark pieces. If you are using stripes, quilt along some of the stripes to accentuate these pieces.

Worlds Without End

Challenging
Pieces per block: 36

A	4 bright
B	16 dark
C	16 light

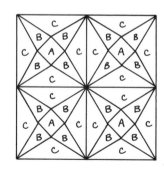

Fig. 103

Templates are on page 55. Wonderful optical illusions can be created by the judicious use of highly contrasting fabrics. One minute you will see 4 stars joined in the middle, the next you'll see a central star within a dark circle of fabric. This is not a block for beginners because of the difficulty of joining the pieces perfectly in the middle, and because insetting is required. Please review *How to Inset*.

The block is assembled in 4 squares. To make each square, sew a B to each edge of A. Inset a C into the space between each of the B pieces. Sew 2 pairs of squares together to make each half of the design.

Press the seam allowances in opposite directions; then sew the halves together to complete the design.

Outline-quilt each of the 4 stars and the A squares.

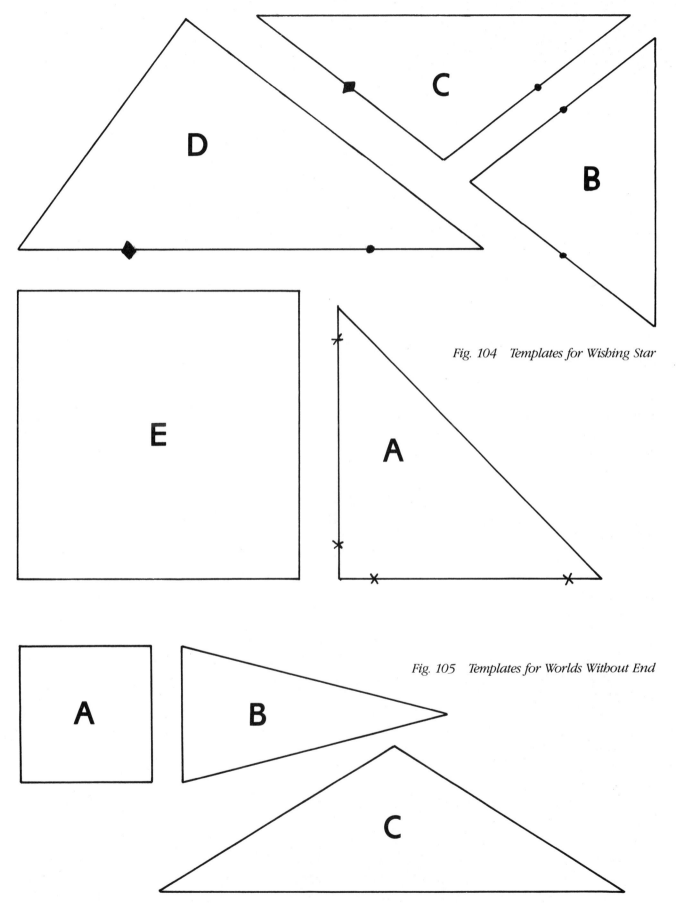

Fig. 104   Templates for Wishing Star

Fig. 105   Templates for Worlds Without End

Block Designs

Because these designs are so simple, I have drawn exploded assembly diagrams for you to follow rather than give the instructions in words. Trace one each of the full-size templates which make up the assembly diagrams and cut out the required number of pieces in each color. Then, sew the pieces together in the numerical order shown in the diagrams.

Bow Tie

Challenging (see How to Inset)
Pieces per block: 5
A   1 bright
B   2 light, 2 dark

Fig. 106

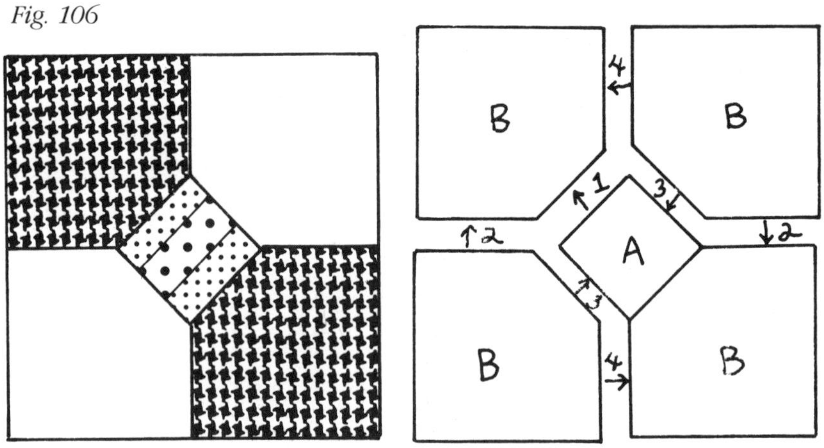

Churn Dash

Easy
Pieces per block: 17
A   4 light, 4 dark
B   4 light, 4 dark
C   1 light

Fig. 107

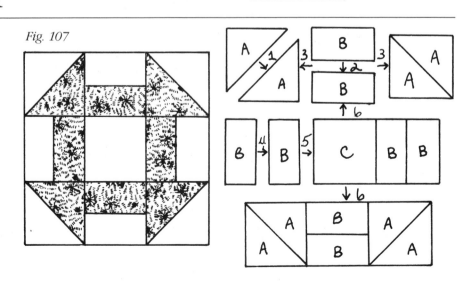

Evening Star

Easy
Pieces per block: 17
A 4 dark
B 8 light
C 4 dark
D 1 light

Fig. 108

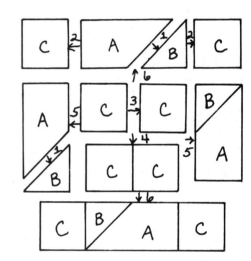

Ladder Steps

Moderate
Pieces per block: 16
A 2 medium,
   2 medium
   reversed
B 4 bright
C 4 light, 4 dark

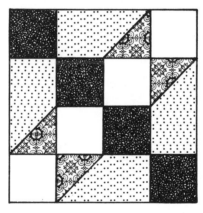

Fig. 109

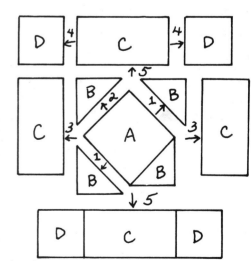

New Album

Easy
Pieces per block: 13
A 1 dark
B 4 light
C 4 medium
D 4 dark

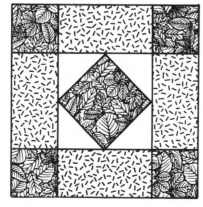

Fig. 110

Right & Left

Fig. 111

Easy
Pieces per block: 9
A   4 light, 4 dark
B   1 bright

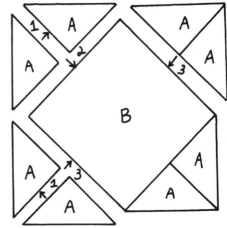

Shoo-Fly

Fig. 112

Easy
Pieces per block: 13
A   4 light, 4 dark
B   4 light, 1 dark

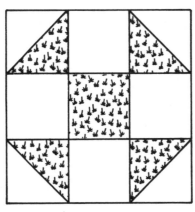
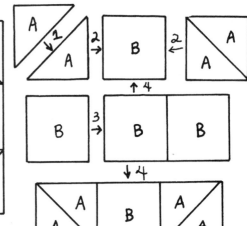

Streak of Lightning

Easy
Pieces per block: 6
A   1 light, 1 light reversed
B   2 dark, 2 dark reversed

Fig. 113

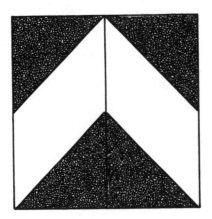
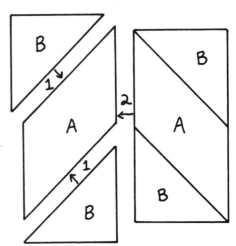

Susannah

Challenging (see How to Inset)
Pieces per block: 9
A   4 bright
B   4 light
C   1 dark

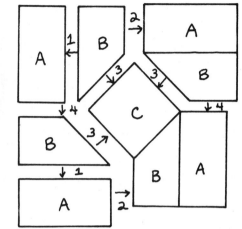

Fig. 114

Variable Star

Easy
Pieces per block: 17
A   4 light, 8 medium
B   4 light
C   1 dark

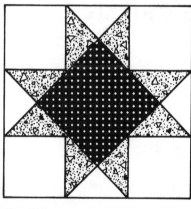

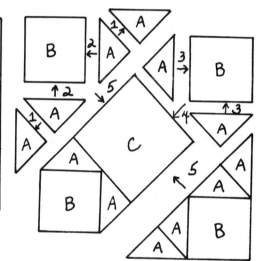

Fig. 115

Windmill

Easy
Pieces per block: 8
A   4 light, 4 dark

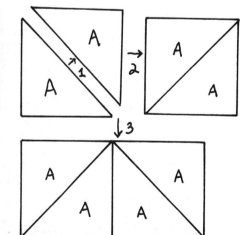

Fig. 116

Beautiful Patchwork Gifts

GIFTS FOR BABIES & CHILDREN

Patchwork Bibs

See color page D.

I received a large number of bibs at my baby shower and remember thinking (back in that carefree pre-baby time!) that I would never use all of them. I changed most of my preconceived notions once the baby was born, and one of the things I realized was that you can never have enough bibs. My daughter is now 2 and we are still using them; only now she likes to pick out the bib that she will wear for each meal. She especially likes the bibs featured here, which must mean that the designs are appealing to those who will actually wear them! I'd like to thank Sharon Falberg, who designed and made these bibs, for allowing me to feature them in this book. The Watermelon Bib is small, and the others are larger.

Before beginning, review the following sections: *Assembling a Project for Quilting*, *Binding a Project* and *Quilt-As-You-Go*.

Fig. 117 An example of the Crazy Bib, design © Sharon Falberg.

60

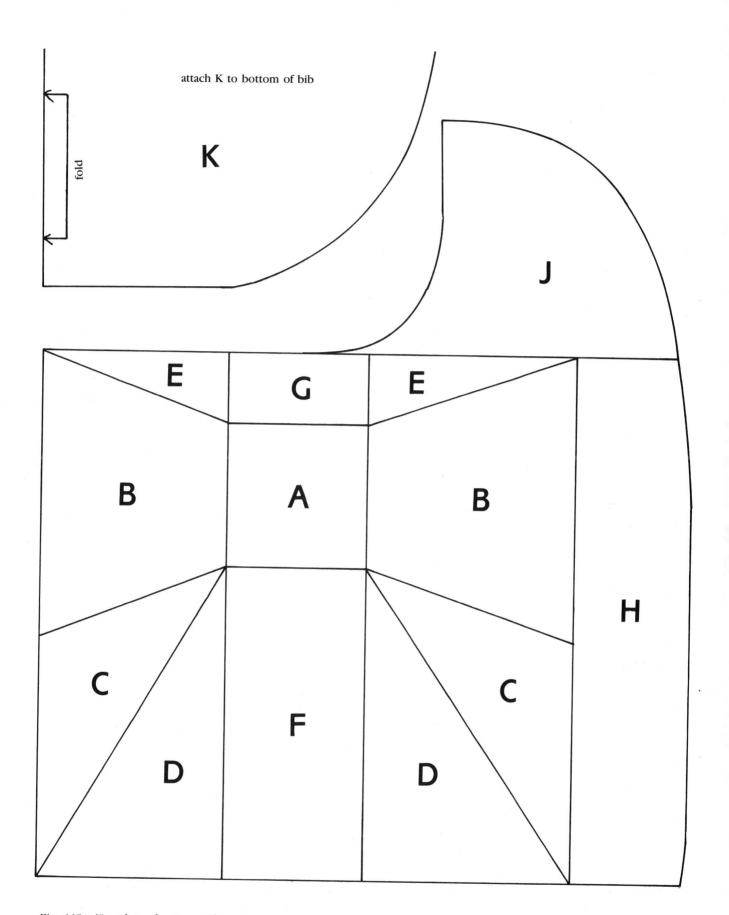

attach K to bottom of bib

fold

K

J

E   G   E

B   A   B

H

C   C

F

D   D

Fig. 118   Templates for Bow Bib

Easy

Finished size: Small 7½" × 8½"; Large 6" × 12"

Requirements

Fabric scrap for bib back: Small 8" × 9"; Large 6½" × 12½"

Batting or 2 layers of thick flannel: Small 8" × 9"; Large 6½" × 12½"

Large fabric scraps in a variety of colors for bib front

Bias binding: Small 1½" × 24" (outer edge) and 1½" × 36" (neck edge); Large 1½" × 34" (outer edge) and 1½" × 36" (neck edge)

Basic Instructions for Making a Bib: Trace the half-pattern for the bib you have chosen, and use this to cut an entire bib back piece and a piece of batting in the same shape. Make the bib front following the individual instructions. Assemble the 3 layers for quilting and baste together. Quilt by hand or machine if desired (this is totally optional); then stitch together around the edges. Trim the edges evenly all around if necessary. Following the instructions for *Binding a Project*, bind the outer edges of the bib, trimming the binding even with each neck edge. Fold the neck edge binding crosswise to find the center; pin to the center neck edge of the bib and bind the neck edge. The excess binding at each side will become the bib's ties. Fold the remaining long raw edge of the binding on each side of the bib to the inside and press so that the fold is even with the other pressed edge. Continue stitching to the end, securing the pressed edges together; turn the raw ends inside and stitch to secure.

WATERMELON BIB

Light pink 1½" × 16"
Medium pink 2" × 16"
Dark pink 1½" × 16"
Green 3" × 16"

Sew the strips together in the order given above; press carefully. Cut the following pieces from fabric, matching the lines on the templates to the strip-pieced fabric where appropriate:

A	1 strip-pieced (place on fold of fabric)	C	1 strip-pieced, 1 reversed strip-pieced
B	1 strip-pieced, 1 reversed strip-pieced	D	1 green, 1 green reversed

Stitch a B section to each side of A; stitch a C to each B; then stitch a D to each end. Mark watermelon seeds on the pink portions of the bib at random, using a permanent black marker pen. Press carefully; then complete the bib as described in *Basic Instructions for Making a Bib*.

BOW BIB

A	1 bright	F	1 light
B	1 bright, 1 bright reversed	G	1 light
C	1 light, 1 light reversed	H	2 light
D	1 bright, 1 bright reversed	J	1 light, 1 light reversed
E	1 light, 1 light reversed	K	1 light (placed on fold of fabric)

Assemble the bow block in 3 vertical strips. For the central strip, sew G and F to opposite sides of A. For the outer strips, sew each C to a D as shown; then sew C and E to opposite sides of each B. Sew the outer strips to the central strip, matching seams carefully. Sew an H to each side of the bow block. Sew each J to the top, matching the outside edges. Sew K to the bottom. If desired, print "Daddy is my beau" on the K piece and embroider the letters in outline stitch using 2 strands of matching embroidery floss. Press carefully; then complete the bib as described in *Basic Instructions for Making a Bib*.

SANTA BIB

A	1 Christmas print, 1 Christmas print reversed	D	1 flesh (placed on fold of fabric)
B	1 red (placed on fold of fabric)	E	1 white, 1 white reversed
C	1 white (placed on fold of fabric)	F	1 white (placed on fold of fabric)

For this bib you'll also need brown embroidery floss and a small white pompon. For the white fabric, try a flannelette to create a fluffy effect.

Assemble the Santa Bib as follows: Sew each A to the angled edge of B. Sew B to C. Sew an E to each angled edge of D. Sew D to C. Sew F to E-D-E. Press carefully. Transfer the curved eye lines to the D piece and embroider in outline stitch using 2

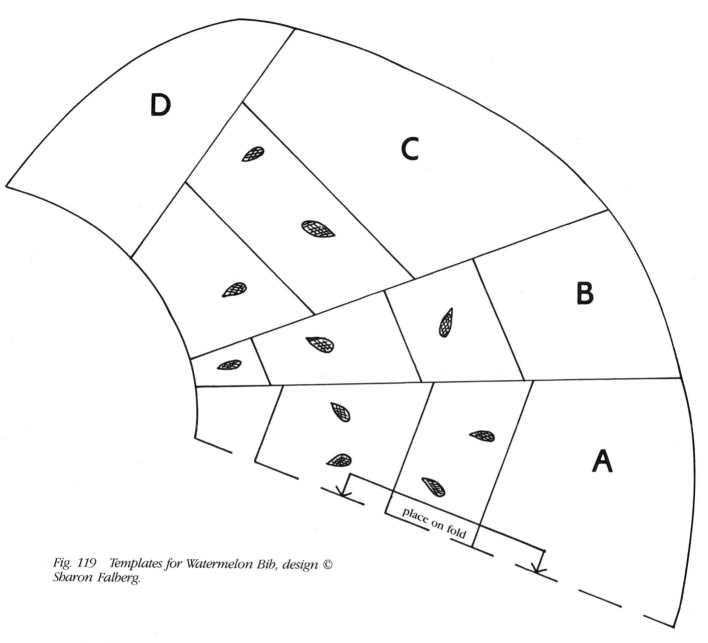

Fig. 119 Templates for Watermelon Bib, design ©
Sharon Falberg.

strands of brown embroidery floss. Stitch the white
pompon to the D/F seam centered evenly between
the side edges at the dot marked on the pattern.
Complete the bib as described in *Basic Instructions
for Making a Bib*.

CRAZY BIB

This can be made in about 10 minutes with the quilt-
as-you-go method. Cut fabric strips to 2¼″ wide and
stitch together, making one very long strip of fabric.
Baste the batting to the wrong side of the bib back.
Baste a shape such as a triangle (shown in the photograph) or a square, right side up, in the middle of
the bib on top of the batting. Following the quilt-as-

you-go method and using your long strip of fabric,
stitch the strip to the central shape, cutting away the
excess after each line of stitching; do not waste any
of the strip, but use the seams as they fall to enhance
the crazy effect. Continue in this way until the entire
bib is covered. The look of the finished design will
depend on your central shape, and no two bibs will
be exactly alike. You can vary the design by placing
the central shape in a corner or along an edge—the
possibilities are endless. When the entire bib is covered, trim the outer edges evenly; then finish the
bib as described in *Basic Instructions for Making a
Bib*. To continue the scrap theme, use the remainder
of your long pieced strip to make the binding.

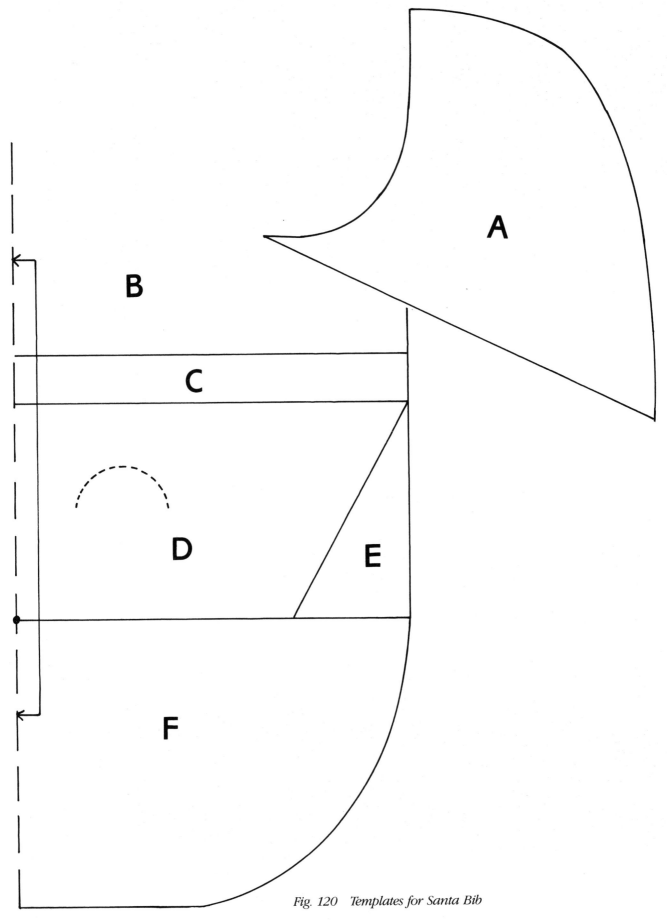

Fig. 120   Templates for Santa Bib

Christmas Clown

Crib Quilt. "The Schoolhouse blocks . . . were hand-pieced during the 1920's or 30's."

B

House Cushion and Doorstop

"This easy-to-make hanger includes a sachet stuffed with potpourri."

Yuletide Stocking, Christmas Tree Ornaments, and a Santa Bib designed by Sharon Falberg.

D

"Snuggle into this gorgeous shawl at Christmas or any other time of the year."

"You can never have enough bibs . . . My daughter especially likes the bibs featured here." Bibs
below designed © Sharon Falberg.

"Maple Leaf Quilt was pieced during the Depression and finished by me."

F

"My husband looked a bit skeptical when I told him I was going to include a patchwork tie in this book. . . . One day he came home from work to see this tie on the bed. 'Now that's a nice tie!' he exclaimed appreciatively."

"This is truly a quick and easy project; I completed the entire article in just a few hours. A Shoe Carrier is unusual but useful."

"Not only will this doll become your child's next best friend, but it will teach little fingers how to use a snap, a button or a zipper, and how to tie a bow."

H

A Patchwork Clock is an unusual gift.

"Enliven a simple dress by wrapping this dazzling creation around your waist!"

I

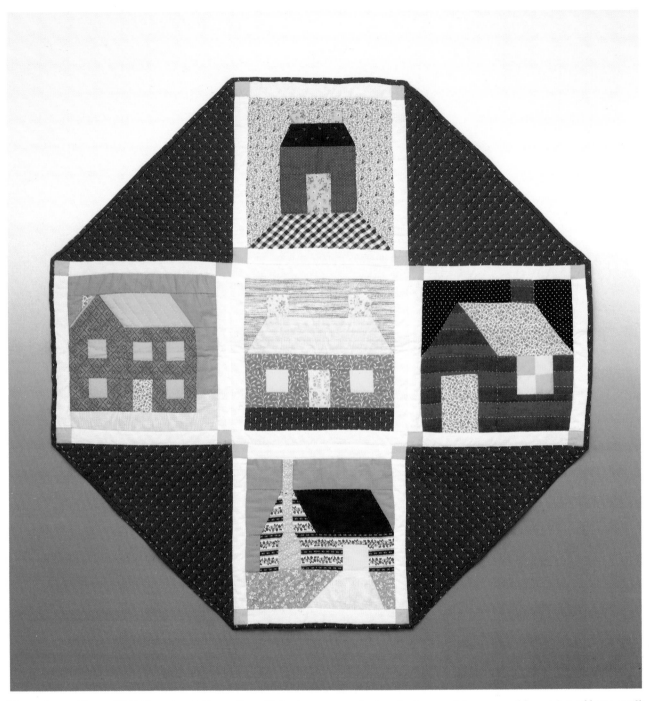

Home Sweet Home Wall Hanging is "a perfect gift for someone who has just moved house and has a lot of bare walls to decorate!"

J

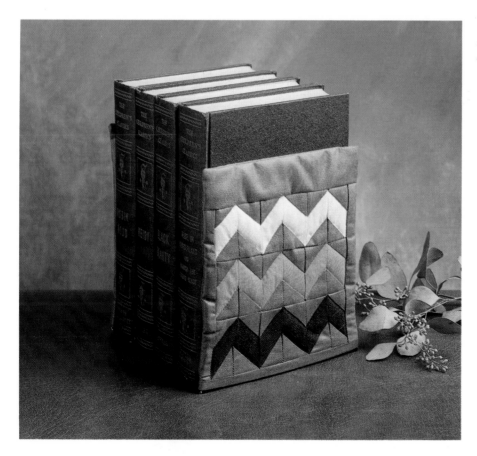

"This colorful Room Tidy will encourage creative play in the cleaning-up process."

L

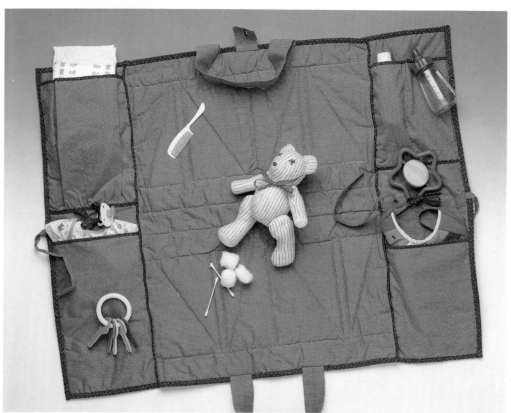

"After juggling my baby all over England and America, I longed for a good serviceable changing bag that would hold everything I need and provide a changing area . . . . I designed one of my own."

"A Harlequin Wall Hanging to grace the recipient's office or workplace."

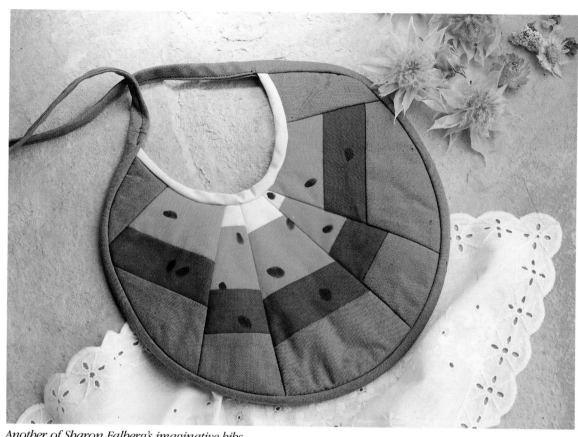

Another of Sharon Falberg's imaginative bibs.

"This footstool will be treasured, particularly if it's made to match a favorite chair."

Ribbon and Bows Tablecloth "will make your table resemble a huge Christmas present."

"Brighten up your kitchen, family room or any other part of your home with these cheerful patchwork pictures."

Baby's Changing Bag

My opinion of mothers who travel—whether it be to a foreign country or just to the local shopping mall—is very high, now that I've become a mother myself. And after juggling my baby all over England and America, I longed for a good serviceable changing bag that would hold everything I need and provide a changing area at the same time. Not finding one of these in any shop, I designed one of my own! I hope you enjoy making and using this bag as much as I do.

Before beginning, review the following sections: *Assembling a Project for Quilting*, *Binding a Project*, *Using a Tube Turner*, *Piping* and *How To Quilt*.

Easy
Size: About 13″ × 20″ (closed); 26″ × 36″ (open)

Requirements
Pieced blocks: 4 10″-square—fabric scraps
Fabric (45″ wide): 1¼ yards; contrasting fabric for binding, piping and inside ties: ⅜ yard
Cord for piping: 1½ yards
Interfacing: ⅛ yard
Plastic for lining bottles pocket: 8½″ × 18½″
Novelty button: 1¾″ diameter

Instructions: To make the outside of the changing bag, select a 10-inch-square design. Piece 4 blocks as directed in the individual instructions. Stitch 2 pairs of blocks together, side by side. Stitch a side block to each side edge of the pieced blocks, matching the 10½″ edges. Following Fig. 121, arrange the pieced/side block pieces and the border strips on a flat surface. (**Note:** If you are using a design such as Regatta, where there is a definite top and bottom to the block, position the blocks so that their bottom edges are sewn to the *middle* border strip.) Stitch the border strips to the blocks. Press carefully.

To make the inside of the changing bag, refer to Fig. 122 during assembly. Before beginning, see *Binding a Project* for instructions on preparing the binding. Also, see *Piping* for instructions on preparing and stitching the piping in place.

Diaper pocket: Cut 2 binding strips, one 10½″ and one 8½″. Bind one edge of the pocket (the top) with the 10½″ piece. Machine-baste the opposite edge of

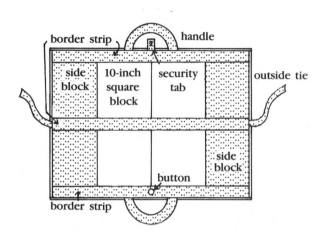

Fig. 121   Diagram showing outside of Baby's Changing Bag

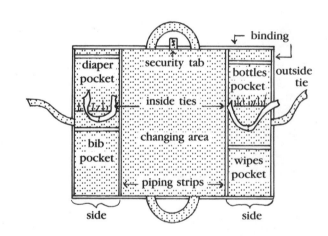

Fig. 122   Diagram showing inside of Baby's Changing Bag

the pocket; pull the basting threads to gather that edge to an 8½″ width. Bind the bottom edge, securing the gathers, with the remaining piece of binding. Pin the pocket to a side piece with the top edge of the pocket 1¼″ below the top edge. Stitch the diaper pocket in place along the bottom and each side edge. If desired, make 2 small pleats along the top edge and press.

Bibs pocket: This pocket can be used to store bibs as well as extra articles of clothing. Cut an 8½″

CUTTING CHART FOR CHANGING BAG		
Name	**Number**	**Measurements**
Side block	*4*	*8½" × 10½"*
Border strip	*3*	*2½" × 36½"*
Batting	*1*	*26½" × 36½"*
Binding (contrasting)	*1*	*1¼" × 167"*
Piping strip (contrasting)	*2*	*1½" × 26½"*
Side	*2*	*8½ × 26½"*
Diaper pocket	*1*	*10½" × 10½"*
Bibs pocket	*1*	*8½" × 12½"*
Bottles pocket	*1*	*8½" × 9½"*
Wipes pocket	*1*	*8½" × 9½"*
Inside tie (contrasting)	*2*	*1" × 12"*
Outside tie	*2*	*1½" × 10"*
Changing area	*1*	*20½" × 26½"*
Security tab	*1*	*2½" × 5½"*
Handle	*2*	*4" × 15"*
Iron-on interfacing	*2*	*3¾" × 14¾"*

length of binding. Bind one short edge of the pocket (the top). Pin the pocket to the side piece (below the diaper pocket) matching the side and bottom edges. Stitch in place along the sides and bottom.

Bottles pocket: Pin the plastic lining to the wrong side of the pocket fabric; half of the lining will be hanging loose from the bottom. Stitch the plastic to the pocket along the top edge. Cut 2 binding strips, one 9½" and one 8½". Bind the top edge of the pocket with the 9½" piece. Fold up the remaining piece of plastic even with the top and stitch along each side edge. Machine-baste along the bottom edge; pull the basting threads to gather that edge to an 8½" width. Bind the bottom edge, securing the gathers, with the remaining piece of binding. Pin the pocket to the remaining side piece with the top edge of the pocket 2¼" below the top edge of the side piece. Find the vertical center of the side piece

and match it to the vertical center of the pocket. Stitch down the exact center, dividing the pocket in half; then stitch in place along the bottom and each side edge.

Wipes pocket: This pocket can be used to store moist towels or a small bottle of lotion and cotton balls. Cut an 8½" length of binding. Bind one short edge of the pocket (the top). Pin the pocket to the side piece (below the bottles pocket) matching the side and bottom edges. Stitch in place along the sides and bottom.

Inside ties: Fold each strip in half lengthwise with right sides facing; stitch the long edges together. See *Using a Tube Turner*. Turn right side out using a tube turner and press with the seam along one edge. Fold the raw edges at each end inside and slip-stitch in place. Find the exact center of each side piece and mark with a dot. Fold each tie in half to find the center; stitch the center of each tie to the marked dot on each side piece. You can use these ties to carry a pacifier, rattle or small toys.

Outside ties: Fold each strip in half with right sides facing; stitch the long edges and one short edge together. Turn right side out using a tube turner and press. Position each tie in the middle of the outer side edge of each side piece; stitch in place, matching raw edges.

Changing area: See *Piping*. Prepare the piping strips as directed; then trim away excess fabric, leaving a ¼″ seam allowance. Stitch the piping to each 26½″ edge of the changing area.

Security flap: Fold strip in half crosswise and stitch each side edge. Turn to the right side and press. Find the center of the 20½″ edge of the changing area and pin in place, matching raw edges. Stitch together securely. Make a ¾-inch vertical buttonhole on the side facing up.

Handles: Center the interfacing on the wrong side of each handle and iron securely in place. Fold each handle in half lengthwise, right sides together, and sew the long edges together. Turn right side out and press with the seam centered on one side. With the nonseamed side facing the changing area and raw edges matching, pin the handles 4″ apart and centered along the top edge. Stitch securely in place.

Assembly: With right sides facing, raw edges even and the piping in between, stitch each side/pockets piece to the changing area. Press carefully.

Next, following instructions in *Assembling a Project for Quilting*, assemble the outside and inside of the changing bag with the batting. Baste the 3 layers together thoroughly; then quilt the patchwork blocks by hand or machine following the individual instructions for the blocks. Stitch around the outer edges and trim off any uneven pieces of batting. Following instructions for *Binding a Project*, bind the long edges of the bag first, securing the handles and security tab in the binding. Then bind the side edges, securing the outer ties in the binding and folding the ends of the binding inside to hide the raw edges. After the binding has been slip-stitched in place, fold the handles, security tab and ties outward; slip-stitch to the edge of the binding to hold in place. Sew a button to the outside of the changing bag, in a position to match the buttonhole on the security flap. Hint: When you give this bag as a gift, or if you intend to use it yourself, remember to include a small terry cloth towel or a piece of plastic to place beneath your baby while changing. Babies are unpredictable, and you wouldn't want to have to wash your bag every time you use it!

Room Tidy

See color page L.

The earlier you can teach your child to keep his or her room tidy, the better! This colorful room tidy will encourage creative play in the cleaning-up process because it will be fun to stuff the various toys, animals and dolls into each of the pockets. Hang this project at child-height to make it easier to use. You can also hang it from the side of a baby's crib and use it to store diapers, wipes and various other essential nursery items. If you can, try to use a different color family for each of the four patchwork blocks (such as the red, blue, yellow and green shown in the color photograph), so that the child can learn to differentiate between colors.

Fig. 123

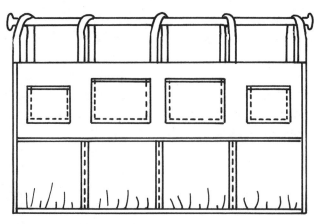

Fig. 124   Diagram of Room Tidy

Before you begin, review the following sections: *Assembling a Project for Quilting, Machine Quilting, Quilt-As-You-Go, Joining Blocks and Binding a Project.*

Easy
Finished size: 20" × 40" (not including handles)
Requirements:
Pieced blocks: 4 10" squares—a variety of bright fabric scraps, such as the primary colors shown in the photograph
Backing for pieced blocks: ⅝-yard neutral fabric such as muslin (fabric A)
Fabric (45" wide): 1¼ yards crisp, sturdy fabric such as chintz in a color to coordinate with the pieced blocks (fabric B); a variety of large fabric scraps in bright colors to match pieced blocks (fabric C); ¼ yard solid bright fabric for binding (fabric D)
Batting
Decorative wooden dowel, about 42" long

Instructions: Select a 10-inch-square design. Piece 4 blocks as directed in the individual instructions. Assemble the blocks for quilting, and quilt each one by machine following the individual instructions. Machine-stitch ⅛ inch away from the outer edges; trim the raw edges neatly. Join the 4 quilted blocks into a row using the *Quilt-As-You-Go: Joining Blocks* method; carefully follow Figures 41–44. Baste a strip of batting to the wrong side of each C divider strip (this will also be called the padded strip). Pin both the A and C divider strips to the same edge of one quilted block: The right side of the A strip should face the back of the block and the right side of the

padded strip should face the front of the block. Stitch together. Open out the padded strip only. Stitch a second block to the opposite long edge of the padded strip with right sides facing. Fold the raw edge of the A strip ¼ inch to the wrong side; smooth over the padded strip and pin so that the folded edge covers the stitching line. Slip-stitch in place securely with matching thread. Continue joining the 4 blocks in this manner. See *Binding a Project*; bind one long edge of the quilted blocks as directed (the top edge). Machine-baste along the lower edge of each of the blocks, breaking the line of stitching at each divider strip.

Prepare each of the upper pockets as follows: With right sides together and raw edges even, stitch 2 pairs of matching pocket pieces together along the short edges and one long edge. Clip corners and turn right side out. Press. Bind the long raw edge of each, folding the raw edges of the binding to the wrong side. Following Fig. 124, pin the upper pockets to the background with the 2 large pockets in the middle, flanked by the small pockets. The bottom edge of each pocket should be 8½ inches below the top edge of the background. Pin the pockets in place carefully, checking to see that they are straight and even. Baste thoroughly in place.

Assemble the background, batting and back for quilting. Mark the placement for the lower pockets as follows: Holding the background horizontally, mark the vertical center using pins. Measure to the right and left of center, just a little over 10 inches; mark with pins. Place the quilted block strip (lower pockets) on the background, matching a divider

CUTTING CHART FOR ROOM TIDY		
Name	**Number**	**Measurements**
Back of pieced blocks (A)	*4*	*10½" × 10½"*
Divider strips (C)	*3*	*1½" × 10½"*
Back/divider strips (A)	*3*	*1½" × 10½"*
Batting	*4*	*10½" × 10½"*
	1	*20½" × 40½"*
	3	*1½" × 10½"*
Binding (D)	*1*	*1½" × 44"*
Small pocket (C: 2 each of 2 different fabrics)	*4*	*6" × 7"*
Small pocket binding (D)	*2*	*1¼" × 7"*
Large pocket (C: 2 each of 2 different fabrics)	*2*	*7" × 9"*
Large pocket binding (D)	*2*	*1¼" × 9"*
Background (B)	*1*	*20½" × 40½"*
Back (B)	*1*	*20½" × 40½"*
Outer binding (D)	*1*	*1½" × 124"*
Hangers (C)	*5*	*2½" × 14"*
Hanger linings (B)	*5*	*2½" × 14"*

strip to each of the 3 pin markings. Thoroughly pin the lower pockets to the background, matching all raw edges and pulling the basting to gather the bottom edge of each block to fit neatly. Pin each divider strip to the background along its entire length; then topstitch each long edge of each divider strip in place, reversing your stitches several times at the top to strengthen the seam. (This stitching will secure the lower pockets to the background, batting and back as well.)

Next, topstitch the pockets to the background, starting in the center of the bottom edge and working up to the top; go back to the center and stitch to the opposite top edge. This may seem like extra work, but I originally stitched from one top edge around the bottom to the other top, and the pockets came out very crooked—probably because of the

batting, the fabric seemed to creep up at the opposite edge, pulling everything out of line!

After the pockets have been stitched in place, smooth the background fabric outward and pin the raw edges together very carefully to prevent the upper layer from shifting during the binding. Bind the outer edges of the project, mitring the corners.

To make the hangers, stitch a lining to each hanger strip with right sides facing together and raw edges even. Stitch together along the two long edges and one short edge. Clip the corners, turn right side out, and press. Fold the raw edges ¼ inch inside and slip-stitch the opening closed. Pin the hangers to the back of the project spaced evenly along the top edge. Slip-stitch in place very securely to the back, and then along the binding edge. Insert a dowel through the loops to hang the project.

Learning Doll

See color page H.

Not only will this doll become your child's next best friend, but it will teach little fingers how to use a snap, a button, or a zipper and how to tie a bow. Choose bright primary colors for the clothes, and yarn to match the child's own hair for the curls! A novelty button, such as the plastic grapefruit button on the doll pictured, will add extra interest.

Before beginning, review the following sections: *Embroidery, Using a Tube Turner* and *Making a Buttonhole.*

Moderate
Size: about 14" tall
Requirements
Pieced blocks: 16 2"-square—fabric scraps
Fabric (45" wide): large scraps of matching fabric for the shirt and sleeves (fabric A); large scrap of flesh-colored fabric for the head and hands (fabric B); scraps of three other contrasting colors for the zipper and pockets (fabric C), belt (fabric D) and shoes (fabric E)
Snaps, one set
Zipper, the shortest you can find (with plastic, not metal, teeth)
Embroidery floss: black; pink, red or orange for the mouth
Novelty button, ½" diameter
Shoelaces, baby-shoe length
Thread to match all the fabrics
Polyester fibrefill
Thick yarn in a color to match the recipient's hair
Large-eyed yarn needle

Instructions: Select one of the following 2-inch-square designs from those featured on pages 56–59: Windmill (shown in the color photograph), Ladder Steps, or Streak of Lightning. Cut out enough pieces for 15 squares. Piece 13 squares following the individual diagram for that design. Piece the remaining 2 squares in halves, but do not sew the halves together. Arrange the pieces on a flat surface as shown in Fig. 126; stitch together in vertical rows with the half squares at the center; then stitch the vertical rows together, matching seams carefully to make each trouser leg. Stitch the uppermost half squares

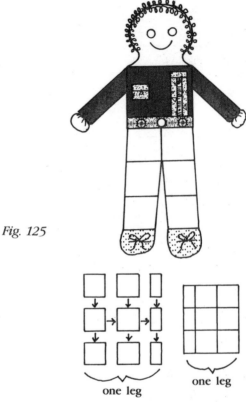

Fig. 125

Fig. 126   Stitch the squares together in vertical rows with the half squares at the center, then stitch the vertical rows together, matching seams carefully, to make each trouser leg.

Fig. 127   Stitch the uppermost half squares together down to the arrow, then stitch the uppermost whole squares together down to the arrow. You now have a circle of fabric with two unjoined strips (legs) extending from the bottom.

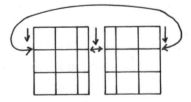

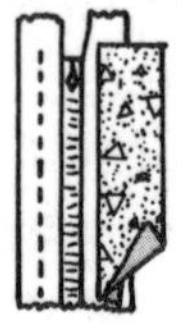

Fig. 128   Place one zipper strip right side down on the zipper with the raw edge of the fabric parallel to and slightly away from the edge of the zipper; stitch together from top to bottom, then turn the fabric to the right side and press.

together down to the arrow as shown in Fig. 127; then stitch the uppermost whole squares together down to the arrow as shown. You now have a circle of fabric with 2 unjoined strips (legs) extending from the bottom. Turn the circle of fabric wrong side out. Adjust the circle so that the seams you have just sewn lie on top of one another; pin together at the lower (crotch) edge, matching the seams carefully. Now, pin each of the legs together, also matching seams carefully. Starting at the bottom edge of one leg, sew up to the crotch, and then back down the other leg. Remove the pins and turn the trousers right side out. Any minor puckers at the crotch will work themselves out once the trousers are stuffed.

Next, make the shirt. Mark the position for the bottom left corner of the pocket on the right side of one shirt piece as follows: Measure ¾ inch in from a side edge (4½-inch edge), and 2¼ inches down from the top edge; lightly mark a dot. Press each raw edge of the pocket ¼ inch to the wrong side; ma-

chine-stitch across one edge (the top edge). Sew one half of the snap near the top edge of the pocket, centered between the side edges. See *How to Appliqué*; appliqué the sides and bottom of the pocket to the shirt, with the bottom left corner of the pocket exactly on the placement dot. Stitch the other half of the snap to the right side of the pocket flap, about ⅜ inch above one 1¾-inch edge and centered between the sides. Fold the pocket flap in half with the snap inside and stitch the side edges together. Turn right side out, fold the raw edges ¼ inch inside and slip-stitch together. Appliqué the top edge of the flap to the shirt so that the snaps match perfectly.

For the zipper, measure 1¼ inches from the side edge (opposite the snap pocket) and draw a line parallel to the side edge. Center the teeth of the zipper on this line so that the top edge of the zipper is 1 inch below the top of the shirt. (**Note:** To cut your zipper to the 3-inch length, measure down 2⅞ inches from the top of the zipper and machine-stitch

CUTTING CHART FOR LEARNING DOLL		
Name	**Number**	**Measurements**
Pieced block	*15*	*2" square*
Shirt (A)	*2*	*4½" × 4¾"*
Snap pocket (C)	*1*	*1½" square*
Snap pocket flap (C)	*1*	*1½" × 1¾"*
Zipper	*1*	*3" long (cut down if necessary)*
Zipper sides (C)	*2*	*1" × 3½"*
Zipper top (C)	*1*	*1" × 1½"*
Belt (D)	*1*	*1½" × 22"*
Head (B)	*2*	*Use pattern (add ¼" seams)*
Sleeves (A)	*2*	*4¼" × 5½"*
Hands (B)	*2*	*2½"-diameter circles*
Shoes (E)	*4*	*Use pattern (add ¼" seams)*

Fig. 129 Template for head pieces

back and forth over the teeth of the zipper several times, using a zigzag stitch if you can. Cut away excess zipper below your stitching.) Stitch the zipper to the shirt about ¼ inch away from the teeth on each side, using a zipper foot on your sewing machine. Next, stitch the zipper sides to the zipper as shown in Fig. 128. Place one zipper strip right side down on the zipper with the raw edge of the fabric strip parallel to and slightly away from the edge of the zipper; stitch together from top to bottom; then turn the fabric right side out and press. Fold the raw edge of the zipper strip under and appliqué to the shirt, covering all raw edges. Repeat for the other side of the zipper. Pull the zipper tab down while you are working on the top. Stitch the 1½-inch edge

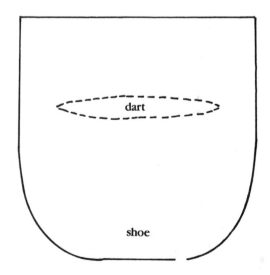

Fig. 130 Template for shoes

72

of the zipper top across the top edge of the zipper and side strips, fold the strip up and press. (Trim off the top edges of the zipper tape as necessary.) Fold the raw edges ¼ inch under and appliqué to the shirt. The raw edges at the bottom of the zipper will be covered by the belt. Stitch the 2 shirt pieces together along the 4½-inch edges with right sides facing and raw edges even, making ¼-inch seams. Do not turn right side out yet.

Insert the trousers inside the shirt, so that the top edge of the trousers matches the bottom edge of the shirt. Pin together all around, adjusting and easing the fabrics together if necessary, and placing the front and back seams of the trousers exactly at the center front and back of the shirt. Stitch together all around. Remove pins and pull the shirt right side out. Stuff the shirt and trousers firmly with fibrefill.

For the belt, fold the fabric in half crosswise with right sides facing; stitch the long edges together. See *Using a Tube Turner*; turn the belt right side out and press. See *Making a Buttonhole*; make a sturdy vertical buttonhole ½ inch away from the folded edge of the belt. Wrap the belt around the body at the waist so that the bottom of the belt just touches the top of the trousers. Pin in place all around so that the buttonhole is above the center front of the trousers. Slipstitch the belt to the body, starting at the raw edge (which will be overlapped and covered by the rest of the belt). Sew each edge of the belt in place; then sew the belt to itself just beyond the raw edges so that they are hidden. Sew a novelty button to the belt beneath the buttonhole.

Next, make the head. Transfer the eyes and mouth to the right side of one head piece. Embroider the eyes in black satin stitch, and the mouth in pink, red or orange outline stitch. Stitch the head pieces together between the X's. Clip into the seam allowance at the curves; then turn right side out. Stuff the head firmly with fibrefill; then insert into the top of the body so that the shoulders are even with the top of the shirt. Fold the top raw edges of the shirt ¼ inch to the inside and pin the folded edge to the shoulders and neck, easing to fit and adding more stuffing if necessary. Slip-stitch the shirt in place all around with tiny invisible stitches.

To make the sleeves, baste across one 4½-inch edge of each sleeve. Sew the 5½-inch edges together, with right sides facing and raw edges even, making a ¼-inch seam. Pull the basting until the end of the sleeve closes; tie the threads into a knot and clip off. Turn each sleeve right side out and stuff until plump. Baste ¼ inch away from the raw edges of each hand circle; pull the basting, gathering the fabric edges together. Stuff the circle with fibrefill; then pull the basting tightly, tie the threads into a knot and clip off. Stitch one hand to the gathered end of each sleeve, hiding all raw edges. Fold the raw edges at the top of the sleeve ¼ inch to the inside and hand-baste all around with matching thread. Pull the basting tightly; then stitch the top of each arm to each side edge of the shirt, just below the neck seam. Sew the arms to the body quite securely, matching the underarm seam to the side seam of the shirt.

Next, make the shoes. Mark the dart on the wrong side of 2 shoe pieces; stitch the dart, tapering your stitches to nothing at each end. Press. Stitch each dart-shoe piece to a plain-shoe piece leaving the straight top edges open. Turn right side out; fold the raw edges at the top ¼ inch to the inside and hand-baste in place all around. Stuff each shoe until plump. Hand-baste around the bottom of each leg; pull the basting gently so that the leg will fit perfectly into the top of each shoe. Insert a leg into each shoe with the dart at the front and slip-stitch together securely. Insert a shoelace into the eye of a yarn needle. Insert the needle through one shoe just above the end of the dart and bring the tip out at the other end of the dart; pull through. This part may be a bit tough—if you need help pulling, use a rubber jar-opener or a bit of deflated balloon to help you. When the shoelace has been pulled through, even up the ends and tie into a bow. Repeat for the other shoe.

To make the hair, insert an 18-inch length of yarn into your yarn needle and make a series of backstitches, but do not pull the backstitches taut; rather, leave them as small loops. Continue in this manner until the entire sides and back of the head have been covered.

Crib Quilt

See color page B.

The Schoolhouse blocks featured in the pictured quilt were hand-pieced during the 1920s or 30s in the midwestern portion of the United States. I purchased the blocks several years ago in an antiques shop in New York City, with the idea that someday they would be the focal point of a child's quilt. I began working on this project when my daughter was about 6 months old and now she's 2 years old, so it's been a "work in progress" for quite some time! Actually, I hadn't finished the quilt deliberately. Because of its size, it was easy to carry around, so it made an excellent demonstration piece when I gave lectures or attended quilt shows and book signings. That is why it may seem familiar to many of you who have met me in the past year or so!

You can make this into a sampler quilt by featuring 6 different blocks, or you can repeat the same block 6 times as I have done. Before beginning, review the following sections: *How to Appliqué, Making Templates, Assembling a Project for Quilting, How to Quilt* and *Binding a Project.*

Easy
Finished size: 40" × 54"

Requirements
Fabric (45" wide): see chart below for yardage
Batting: 41½ × 55½" piece

Instructions: For the quilt top, select a 10-inch-square design. Piece 6 blocks following the individual instructions. The block used for the quilt in the photograph is called Schoolhouse; instructions are on page 43. (**Note:** If you wish, you can choose 6 different block designs and make a sampler-style quilt.) Sew a vertical frame to each side of each block. Sew a horizontal frame to the top and bottom of each block.

Arrange the blocks on a flat surface in 3 rows with 2 blocks in each row. When you are satisfied with the arrangement, sew a short sash between each block, forming 2 vertical strips as shown in Fig. 132. Next, join the 2 vertical strips by sewing the long edges to each side of the long sash. Sew a vertical border to each side edge of the pieced blocks. Sew a horizontal border to the top and bottom edges.

Fig. 131

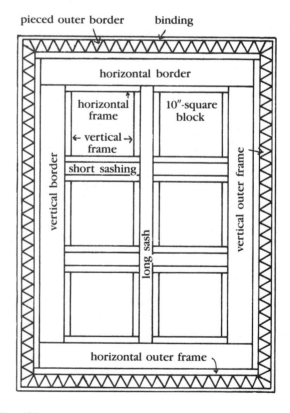

Fig. 132

74

Sew a vertical outer frame to the side edges; then sew a horizontal outer frame to the top and bottom edges.

For the pieced outer border, arrange your triangles so that the darker triangles are touching the frame and the lighter triangles form the outer edge of the quilt; see Fig. 131. When you are satisfied with the arrangement, sew the triangles together in 4 long strips with 37 triangles each for the top and bottom strips and 51 triangles for each side strip. Sew the triangle strips to the top, bottom and sides of the quilt. Press very carefully, spreading the seam allowances at each of the 4 corners outward so that they overlap slightly. Fold the long edges of the B corner pieces ¼ inch to the wrong side and press. Appliqué the corners to the quilt using matching thread, sewing with very tiny invisible stitches at the sharp point of each corner; see *How to Appliqué*. Press the quilt top very carefully.

See *Making Templates*. Construct a sturdy template for the feather border and corner (or create your own quilting pattern to fill the border). Using a hard-lead pencil or other marking device, trace around the template to transfer the design to each

CUTTING CHART FOR CRIB QUILT			
Name	**Number**	**Measurements**	**Yardage**
Pieced blocks	6	10½" × 10½"	⅜ yard each of 5 or more fabrics
FRAME FOR BLOCKS *Vertical frame* *Horizontal frame*	 12 12	 1½" × 10½" 1½" × 12½"	⅛ yard*
SASHING *Short sash* *Long sash*	 4 1	 2½" × 12½" 2½" × 40½"	1¼ yards (includes fabric for inner borders)
INNER BORDERS *Vertical border* *Horizontal border*	 2 2	 4½" × 40½" 4½" × 34½"	See above
OUTER FRAME *Vertical outer frame* *Horizontal outer frame*	 2 2	 1½" × 48½" 1½" × 36½"	1⅜ yards*
PIECED OUTER BORDER *Triangles (A)* *Corners (B)*	 176 4	 Use pattern piece Use pattern piece	Large variety of scraps in darks and lights
Back	1	41½" × 55½"	1⅝ yards
Binding	1	1½" × 192"	¼ yard*

*Note: If you are making the block frames, outer frame and binding out of the same fabric, you only need buy a total of 1⅜ yards.

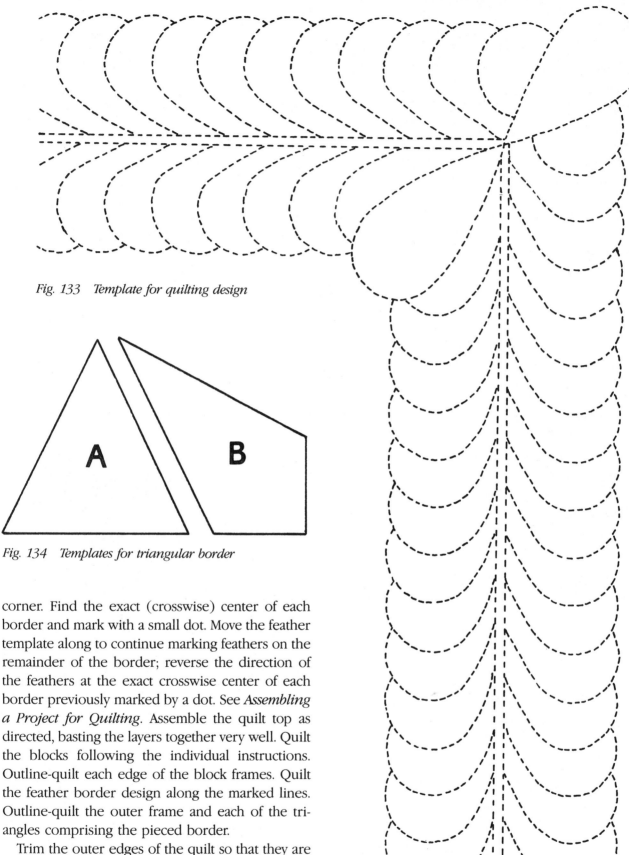

Fig. 133   *Template for quilting design*

Fig. 134   *Templates for triangular border*

corner. Find the exact (crosswise) center of each border and mark with a small dot. Move the feather template along to continue marking feathers on the remainder of the border; reverse the direction of the feathers at the exact crosswise center of each border previously marked by a dot. See *Assembling a Project for Quilting*. Assemble the quilt top as directed, basting the layers together very well. Quilt the blocks following the individual instructions. Outline-quilt each edge of the block frames. Quilt the feather border design along the marked lines. Outline-quilt the outer frame and each of the triangles comprising the pieced border.

Trim the outer edges of the quilt so that they are even. Review *Binding a Quilt* for instructions on making and attaching the binding. Bind the quilt all around, mitring the corners.

PRESENTS FOR WOMEN

Seminole Patchwork Belt

See color page I.

Enliven a simple dress by wrapping this dazzling creation around your waist! It looks complicated, but by using the Seminole Patchwork method employed by the Seminole Indians, you can whip this up in no time. I actually purchased the patchwork portion of the belt (by the yard) when I visited a Miccosukee Indian Reservation in Florida.

Before beginning, review the following sections: *Assembling a Project for Quilting* and *Machine Quilting.*

Moderate
Size: To fit the wearer; see directions below
Requirements
Fabric (45" wide): ⅛ yard each of a light and bright fabric; ⅜ yard of a dark fabric.
Batting: 2½" wide × the wearer's waist measurement

Instructions: To make the Seminole Patchwork, follow Figs. 136–139. Cut two ⅝-inch by 44-inch strips of the bright fabric. Then cut two 2½-inch by 44-inch strips each of the light and dark fabrics. Following Fig. 136, sew the light and dark fabrics to opposite sides of the bright fabric strip, making 2 pieced strips. Next, using a ruler, measure and mark off ⅝-inch-wide pieces across each strip; cut along each marked line. Then, arrange your pieces alternately following Fig. 137. Sew the strips together

Fig. 135

matching the seams indicated by the arrows in Fig. 138. Your pieced strip should look like Fig. 139. As you are stitching the pieced strip, measure the length from time to time, and continue joining pieces until the strip measures the same as the wearer's waist. Using a ruler and pencil, draw a straight line across the top and bottom of the pieced strip to eliminate the staggered edges; make sure that the width of the piece you have marked is 2½ inches. Trim off the excess fabric along the marked lines. Press gently because the strip is now on the bias and will tend to stretch.

For the back, cut a strip of the dark fabric 3½ inches wide and the same length as the pieced strip.

Assemble the Seminole patchwork, the batting and the back for quilting, centering the batting and the patchwork evenly between the long edges of the back. Following the quilting pattern in Fig. 139, machine-quilt the patchwork in one continuous line of stitching, starting at one short end and working to the opposite one. Machine-stitch ¼ inch away from each raw edge of the patchwork. Trim away any excess batting extending beyond the edges. Fold each long edge of the back ¼ inch to the wrong side. Fold again so that the edge of the back covers the outer line of stitching on the patchwork; pin the folded edge to the right side of the patchwork and slipstitch in place invisibly.

For the ties, cut 4 strips of the dark fabric 3½ inches wide and 2 inches longer than the wearer's waist measurement; 2 strips will be the ties and 2 strips will become the tie facings. With right sides together and raw edges even, stitch each tie to a tie facing at the long edges. Taper your stitching lines to form a point at one short edge; at the other short edge, leave ¼ inch unstitched at the end of each line of stitching. Trim away excess fabric at the point, leaving a ¼-inch seam allowance; clip off the corner point; then turn right side out and press carefully.

Next, secure the tie to the patchwork. With right sides facing and raw edges even, stitch each tie to the patchwork, holding the tie facing out of the way so as not to catch it in your stitching. Fold the raw edge of the facing ¼ inch inside and slipstitch in place, covering the line of stitching.

Topstitch all around the edge of each tie to finish. To wear the belt, wrap it around the waist with the patchwork in front. Crisscross the ties at the back and bring them back to the front. Tie the ends into a small knot and hide the knot and ties under the patchwork portion of the belt.

You can also tie the belt in the fashion shown in the color photograph on page I.

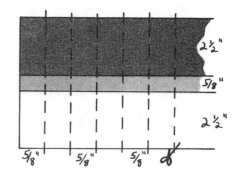

Fig. 136

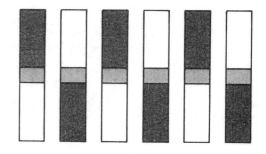

Fig. 137

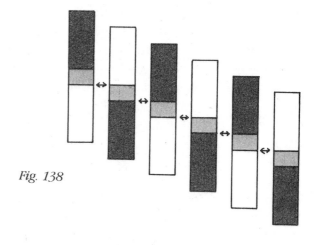

Fig. 138

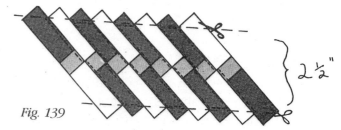

Fig. 139

Padded Hanger with Sachet

See color page C.

Take care of your valuable clothes by storing them on a softly padded hanger. Your garments and closet will be filled with a lovely scent because this easy-to-make hanger includes a sachet stuffed with potpourri that is stitched to one side.

Before beginning, review the following sections: *How to Appliqué* and *Using a Tube Turner*.

Easy
Size: About 7½" high × 16" wide
Requirements
Pieced block: 2" square—fabric scraps
Fabric (45" wide): ¼ yard
Contrasting fabric for bow: 1¼" × 20" strip
Batting: 2 6" × 17" pieces plus a 1" × 6" scrap
Wire hanger, standard size (about 7½" high × 16" wide)
Potpourri: small amount

Instructions: Select a 2-inch-square design from those featured on pages 56–59; piece one square following the individual diagram. Press the outer edges of the square ¼ inch to the wrong side. Set aside.

To make the padded fabric cover, cut 2 pieces of fabric about 1 inch larger all around than your hanger. Place the lower portion of the hanger on the wrong side of one fabric piece as shown in Fig. 141. Using a pencil, trace around the outside of the hanger; then draw a second line ¼ inch away from the first line all around. Cut out the fabric along the outer marked line; use this piece as a pattern to cut out the second fabric piece and two pieces of batting. Save the leftover fabric pieces. Place the 2-inch square on the right side of one piece of fabric, centered between the side edges, and either close to the top point as shown in the assembly diagram or about 1¼ inches lower down. See *How to Appliqué*; appliqué the square to the fabric, leaving a 1-inch opening along the bottom edge. Carefully stuff potpourri into the opening until the square is plump; then continue stitching the remainder of the square to the fabric. Baste the batting to the wrong side of each fabric piece.

Following Fig. 142, pin the fabric pieces together

Fig. 140

with right sides facing and raw edges even; the batting will be on the outside of the pieces you are sewing together, but you should have no trouble getting it through your machine. Stitch the pieces together, starting at the curved bottom edge and working your way up to the top point. Stop your stitching about ½ inch away from the top point as

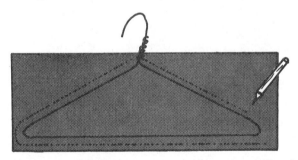

Fig. 141   Place the wire hanger on the wrong side of the fabric and trace all around; draw a second line ¼" away from the first.

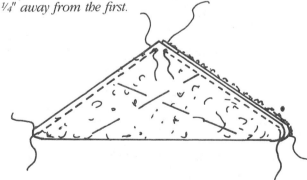

Fig. 142   Stitch the padded fabrics together with right sides facing and raw edges even, making a ¼" seam; stop stitching about ½" away from the point on each side.

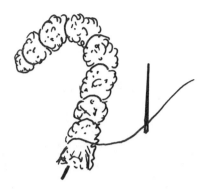

Fig. 143   Wrap the batting around the hook and secure it to the wire by wrapping and sewing it, using a needle and thread.

Fig. 144

shown in Fig. 142. Turn right side out, keeping the raw edges inside at the top point so that you have a finished squared edge at the top.

Next, pad the hook portion of the hanger following Fig. 143. Take the remaining strip of batting and wrap it around the hook; secure the batting to the wire by wrapping and stitching it in place with a needle and thread. Cut a bias strip of fabric 1½″ × 7″ to match your fabric cover; cut this strip from the remaining fabric along the angled edge where one of the hanger pieces was previously cut out. Press one long edge ¼ inch to the wrong side. Wrap the fabric lengthwise around the padded hook and stitch the pressed edge on top of the unpressed edge using matching thread and making small stitches. This part will take a bit of time, and I suggest that you work from the bottom edge to the tip of the hook so that you already have an established line of stitching before you get to the curved area. (Also, leave any excess fabric hanging at the bottom edge of the hook.) Fold the raw edges at the tip inside and stitch in place securely.

Next, insert the padded and fabric-covered hook through the opening in the padded fabric cover. Arrange the fabric cover over the hanger so that the seams are centered on the wire at the sides. Fold the raw edges at the bottom of the hanger inside, lapping the front edge over the back. Slip-stitch in place. If necessary, you can bend the wire at the bottom upwards so that you have an easy fit. Slip-stitch the folded edge at the top of the cover to the excess fabric that is hanging down from the hook.

Next, make the bow with the strip of contrasting fabric (use one of the fabrics you selected for your 2-inch-square block). Stitch the long edges together with right sides facing together, making a ¼-inch seam. Using a tube turner, turn right side out and press with the seam centered on one side. Fold the raw ends inside and slip-stitch in place. Tie this fabric into a pretty bow around the base of the hook. Slip-stitch to the fabric underneath so that the bow won't shift (Fig. 144).

Patchwork Photograph Frame

See color page K.

Enhance a much-loved photograph by framing it in patchwork. Make the frame in fabrics to match the room for which it is intended—an excellent gift for a new mother, grandmother or a newly married couple. Be careful to choose neutral fabrics for the inner border (the A, B and C pieces), so that they do not compete with the photograph. For the 4 outer corners (the F pieces), you can choose one of the 2-inch-square designs on pages 56–59 as shown in the color photograph, or you can simply use plain squares as shown in the assembly diagram.

Although the patchwork is not that difficult (the inner border is a bit tricky, though), I have called this a challenging project because it took me quite a while to attach the patchwork to the frame; it really just requires patience and I haven't got a lot of that! If you are very good with other types of arts and crafts, you should have no trouble with this project.

Challenging
Size: 8¾" × 10¾"; to frame a 4" × 6"
photograph
Requirements
Fabric scraps in solids and prints for the patchwork; ⅜ yard matching fabric for back of frame and stand
Batting: 8¾" × 10¾"
Sturdy cardboard: two 8½" × 10½" pieces and a piece for the stand (see full-size template for stand)
Utility knife
Metal-edged ruler
Fabric glue
Tape

Instructions: To make the patchwork portion of the frame, cut the following from fabric:

A	4 medium	F	4 2"-
B	2 light		patchwork
C	2 light		squares, or 4
D	2 dark		bright
E	2 dark		

Fig. 145   Photograph frame 8¾" × 10¾"

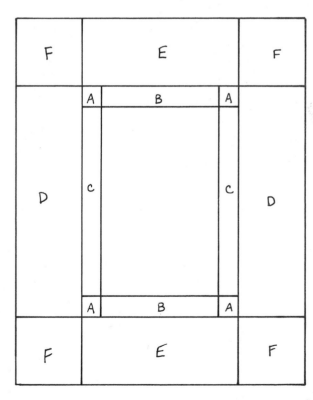

Fig. 146   Assembly diagram

For the inner border, sew the A, B and C pieces together, leaving the ¼-inch seam allowances un-stitched at each inner corner as follows: First, care-fully mark ¼-inch seam allowances on the wrong side of the 4 A pieces (Fig. 147). Arrange the A, B and C pieces on a flat surface so that you can deter-mine which edges will become the inner corners. Stitch an A to the short edge of each B, stopping your stitching ¼ inch away from the inner corner where A will be sewn to C; see Fig. 148 and Fig. 149. Next, stitch each A to C, being careful to stop your stitching at the inner corner's seam allowance; see Fig. 150. The inner border is now finished. (**Note:** You are leaving the seam allowances free at the in-ner edges of the border so that you can secure them to the back of the cardboard when assembling the frame.)

Stitch D to each A-C-A. If you are making the F pieces in patchwork, assemble those following the individual diagram for the block. Stitch F to each end of each E. Stitch E-F-E to the central portion of the frame, matching seams carefully, to complete the patchwork. Next, cut 4 facings from the dark fabric: 2 side facings 11¼″ × 2″ and 2 top and bottom fac-ings 9¼″ × 2″; carefully mark the seam allowances along the short edges of these strips. Stitch the fac-ings to the sides and top and bottom edges of your patchwork, between the marked seam allowances; do not stitch into the seam allowances at the short ends. Press carefully, pressing the outer seam al-lowances of the patchwork towards the facings. Press the seam allowances along the inner border ¼ inch to the wrong side.

Trace rectangle G and transfer to the middle of one piece of cardboard. Using a utility knife, cut out the central rectangle. Use the rectangle pattern to cut out the middle portion from your piece of bat-ting as well. Glue the batting to one side of the cardboard and let dry thoroughly.

While you are waiting for the glue to dry, prepare the frame back and the stand. Trim about ⅛ inch away from each edge of the remaining cardboard rectangle (this is so that the edges of the back are not visible from the front). Cut out a 10¾″ × 12¾″ piece of fabric. Center the cardboard on the wrong side of the fabric and run fabric glue around the edges of the cardboard (on the side facing up).

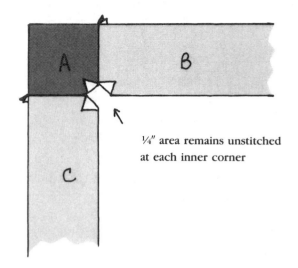

¼″ area remains unstitched
at each inner corner

Fig. 147

Fig. 148

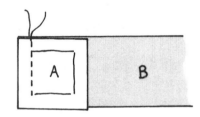

Fig. 149

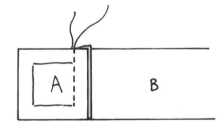

Fig. 150

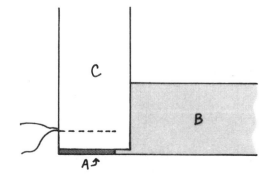

Fig. 151

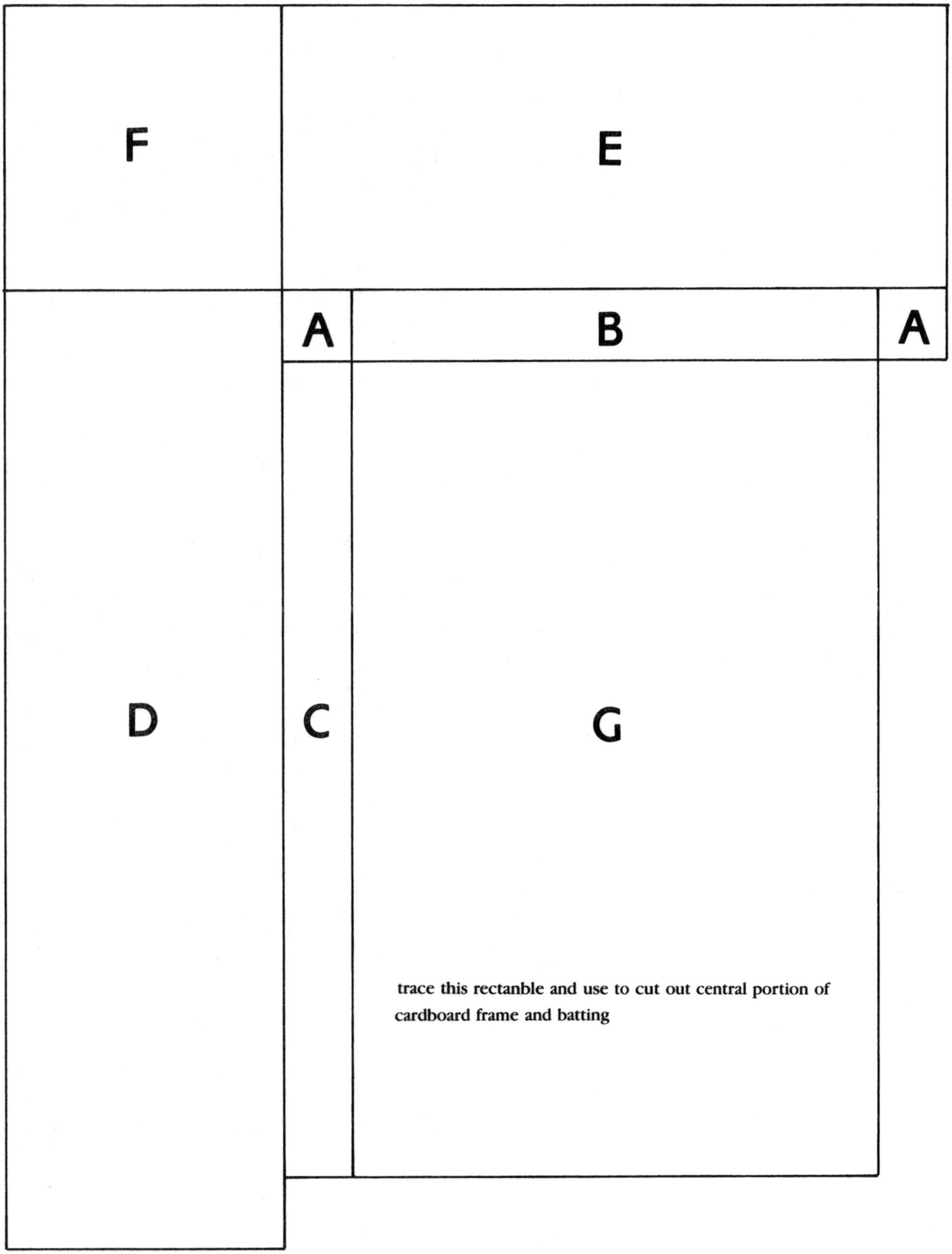

F

E

A

B

A

D

C

G

trace this rectanble and use to cut out central portion of cardboard frame and batting

Fig. 152   Templates for frame

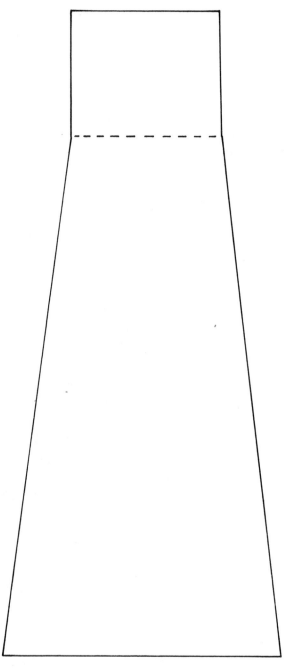

Fig. 153   Templates for stand

Wrap the raw edges of the fabric neatly onto the cardboard and glue in place. Let dry. Cut a piece of matching fabric 8½″ × 10½″; press each of the raw edges ½ inch to the wrong side. Center on the cardboard rectangle and glue in place so that it covers all the raw edges of the other piece of fabric; this will be the side that is glued to the front.

To make the stand, trace the full-size pattern and use to cut one stand from sturdy cardboard. Score the cardboard along the dash lines by running your utility knife lightly along the cardboard a few times; do not cut all the way through. Neatly cover the stand with a scrap of fabric, gluing it securely in place with the seam centered on the *unscored* side of the stand.

By now the glued batting should have dried and you can attach the patchwork. This is the tricky part, so have patience—it will work! Gently place the patchwork on top of the batting and wrap the raw edges to the back of the cardboard. Hold the edges with tape while you are working. Make sure that the corners are straight and that the seam line of the facings is exactly on the edge of the cardboard. Fold the raw edges of the inner border to the back of the cardboard and tape in place. (**Note:** I found that I had to trim the edges of the inner rectangle ever so slightly for a perfect fit. Just don't trim the opening wider than 4″ × 6″ or you'll have to use a larger photograph!) Continue gently smoothing and stretching the patchwork over the batting and cardboard until it is perfect; then glue in place to the back of the cardboard. Let dry thoroughly; then remove the tape.

Glue the front to the back along one short and two long edges. Bend the top flap of the stand along the score line; glue the bent area to the back of the frame so that the frame will stand either horizontally or vertically—your choice. Insert a photograph through the unglued side and center within the opening; hold the photograph in place with a small piece of tape so that the photograph can be changed at some later date if desired.

Circular Patchwork Pictures

See color page P.

Fig. 154

Brighten up your kitchen, family room or any other part of your home with these cheerful patchwork pictures. They are excellent gift items because they take so little time to make, and they will add a lovely spot of color to any wall. The plastic hoop-style frames that are used here can be found in many crafts shops as well as your local patchwork and quilting shop.

Before beginning, review *Assembling a Project for Quilting.*

Easy, Moderate and Challenging
Size: 7"-diameter design, to fit into an 8"-diameter frame
Requirements
Fabric: scraps in solids and prints for the patchwork; 12"-diameter circle of matching fabric for back; 12½"-diameter circle of muslin if quilting
Batting (optional): 12½"-diameter circle
Decorative plastic (or wooden) hoop: 8" diameter along outside edge. If hoop has a decorative hanging loop, then you'll need a decorative hook secured to the wall; if hoop has plain edges, you'll need a large "eye" from a hook-and-eye set and some hanging device such as a nail or small hook secured to the wall.

Instructions: Select one of the 3 designs that follow and complete the patchwork as directed in the individual instructions. If you plan to quilt the patchwork, assemble the project for quilting; quilt the design by hand or machine following the individual instructions for the design.

Trim the back and the batting even with the edges of the patchwork. Center the patchwork on top of the inside ring of the hoop. Carefully press the outer ring in place, being sure that the patchwork is evenly centered within the outer ring. Thread a large needle with sturdy thread; knot the end. Baste close to the raw edges of the patchwork at the back of the hoop, pulling the thread tightly as you sew to gather the raw edges evenly. Continue all the way around; then work a second row of basting, ¼ inch away from the first. Knot the end.

Machine-baste ¼ inch away from the raw edges of the back fabric. Pull the basting gently to gather the fabric to fit over the back of the patchwork. Test the fit; when satisfied that all raw edges will be neatly covered, press the back. Pin to the back of the patchwork; slip-stitch in place.

If you have a frame with a hanging loop at the top, simply secure a decorative hook to the wall and hang your project. If you have a plain hoop, sew a large "eye" to the back of the project quite close to the top; hang from a small hook or nail in the wall.

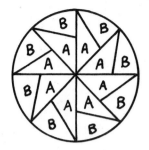

Fig. 155

Spinning Star
Easy
Pieces per block: 16
A   4 bright
    reversed, 4
    dark reversed
B   8 light reversed

Stitch each A to B. Arrange the pieces on a flat surface, alternating the bright and dark A's. Stitch each dark A to a bright A-B edge, making 4 quarters. Stitch 2 pairs of quarters together to complete each half of the design. Stitch the 2 halves together to complete the design, being careful to match the seams carefully in the middle.

Fig. 156

Circular Star
Moderate
Pieces per block: 32

A	4 light, 4	C 8 light
	medium	D 8 light
B	4 bright, 4	
	dark	

Assemble the patchwork in 4 quarters; each quarter is composed of 2 triangles. To make each triangle, stitch C to each B, matching the **X**'s. Then, stitch each D to B-C, matching the dots. To complete the triangles, stitch each dark B to a light A; stitch each bright B to a medium A.

Arrange the triangles on a flat surface, alternating colors as shown in the assembly diagram. To make the 4 quarters of the design, stitch 4 pairs of triangles together, stitching each light A triangle to a medium A triangle. Stitch 2 pairs of quarters together to complete each half of the design. Stitch the 2 halves together to complete the design, being careful to match the seams in the middle.

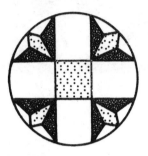
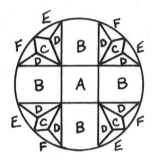

Fig. 157

Tulips
Challenging
Pieces per block: 25

A	1 dark	E	4 light
B	4 light	F	4 light
C	4 bright		
D	4 dark, 4 dark		
	reversed		

Assemble the patchwork in 3 horizontal strips. To construct the middle strip, stitch a B to opposite sides of A. To construct the top and bottom strips, first complete each tulip. Stitch a D to opposite sides of C. Review *How to Inset*. Inset E into the seam formed by C-D; inset F in the remaining seam formed by C-D. Stitch a tulip to each side of the remaining two B's. Stitch the three strips together, matching seams carefully, to complete the design. Quilt the central A block in the pattern given on the template.

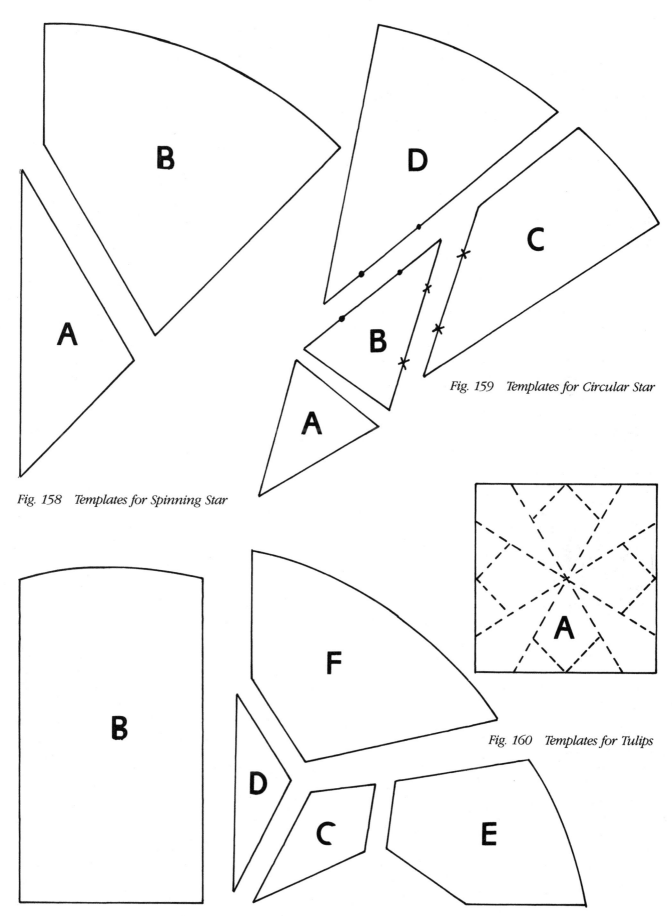

Fig. 158 Templates for Spinning Star

Fig. 159 Templates for Circular Star

Fig. 160 Templates for Tulips

87

Patchwork Clock

See color page I.

Easy
Size: 7"-diameter design, to fit into an 8"-diameter frame

Requirements

Fabric: scraps in solids and prints for the patchwork; 12"-diameter circle of matching fabric for back; 12½"-diameter circle of muslin or other plain fabric

Batting: 12½"-diameter circle

Purchased battery-operated clock mechanism, with minute hand no longer than 4"; depth of the mechanism should be no greater than ½"

Decorative plastic or wooden hoop: 8" diameter along outside edge.

If hoop has a decorative hanging loop, then you'll need a decorative hook secured to the wall; if hoop has plain edges, you'll need a large "eye" from a hook-and-eye set and some hanging device such as a nail or small hook secured to the wall.

Instructions: Select one of the 3 circular designs on the previous pages and complete the patchwork as directed in the individual instructions. If you select the Spinning Star or Circular Star design, do not complete the stitching in the middle; allow a small hole, large enough to accommodate the post from the clock mechanism, to remain open. If you select Tulips, mark a dot in the exact center of A and cut an **X** in the fabric over the dot. Fold the raw edges to the wrong side, leaving a hole large enough to fit the post from the clock mechanism; slip-stitch the raw edges to the wrong side invisibly. Assemble the project for quilting; at the center, cut away a ½-inch-diameter circle of muslin and batting. Quilt the design by hand or machine following the individual instructions. (**Note:** Quilting the patchwork design is entirely optional; I didn't quilt my clock. However, the back and batting are required to support the clock mechanism.)

Trim the back and batting even with the edges of the patchwork. Center the patchwork on top of the inside ring of the hoop. Carefully press the outer ring in place, being sure that the patchwork is evenly centered within the outer ring. Remove the small screw securing the hands to the clock mecha-

Fig. 161

nism and remove hands. Insert the post of the mechanism through the hole in the center of your patchwork from the wrong side. Carefully re-attach the hands and screw, making sure that the hands are raised away from the patchwork enough so that their movement isn't hindered. Thread a needle with sturdy doubled thread. Sew the movement to the back of the patchwork as best you can, being sure that your stitches don't show on the right side. You should be able to make several stitches through the area where the battery is inserted, but also make several long stitches over the entire mechanism.

Thread a large needle with sturdy thread; knot the end. Baste close to the raw edges of the patchwork at the back of the hoop, pulling the thread tightly as you sew to gather the raw edges evenly. Continue all the way around; then work a second row of basting, ¼ inch away from the first. Knot the end.

Machine-baste ¼ inch away from the raw edges of the back fabric. Pull the basting gently to gather the fabric to fit over the back of the patchwork. Test the fit; when satisfied that all raw edges will be neatly covered, press the back. Replace the fabric on the back of the clock and find the area on the mechanism where the battery will be inserted. Cut a hole in the back large enough to fit the battery; fold the raw edges to the wrong side and slip-stitch in place. Pin the fabric circle to the back of the patchwork with the opening positioned over the battery area; slip-stitch in place.

If you have a frame with a hanging loop at the top, simply secure a decorative hook to the wall and hang your project. If you have a plain hoop, sew a large "eye" to the back of the project quite close to the top; hang from a small hook or nail in the wall.

MEMENTOS FOR MEN

String Patchwork Tie

See color page G.

My husband looked a bit skeptical when I told him I was going to include a patchwork tie in this book. "I can't really see a man wanting to wear patchwork around his neck," he declared. I said nothing more about it and one day he came home from work to see this tie on the bed. "Now that's a nice tie!" he exclaimed appreciatively. His look of delight with his "gift" turned to sheepishness when he realized it was made in patchwork. I consider that a success story! I hope you enjoy making and giving this tie as much as I did.

Easy
Size: 54" long, about 3" wide at the bottom
Requirements
Base: 1 8" × 56" soft fabric such as muslin (can be pieced as necessary because it won't be seen)
Main Fabric: 1 strip, 1¼" wide × 6" long; 30 strips, each 1" wide × about 8" long; 1 6" × 25" piece for tail—¾ yard
Fabric for stripes: 4 contrasting fabrics to make 7 strips, each ¾" wide × about 8" long
Large sheet of soft paper, such as newspaper, for the pattern
Long ruler
Pencil
Spray starch

Instructions: For the pattern, you'll need a sheet of paper about 8 inches wide and 55 inches long, so tape pieces of soft paper together to obtain this length. Following the tie diagram, Fig. 165, and the patterns for the front tip and tail of the tie, draw the pattern on the paper using a ruler for accuracy. The pattern you have drawn is the finished size of the

Fig. 162

tie. Now add a 1½-inch facing to each side edge (facings are included in the full-size patterns for the front tip and the tail); do not add a facing to the angled ends.

Using your complete pattern, cut out a base from soft fabric; you do not need to add any seam allowances. Iron the fabric well using spray starch to give it some body. Place the 1¼"-wide strip of the main fabric right side up on the base, even with the angled edge of the front tip; see the actual size pattern (Fig. 163) for placement. Stitch the outer edges together. With right sides facing and raw edges even,

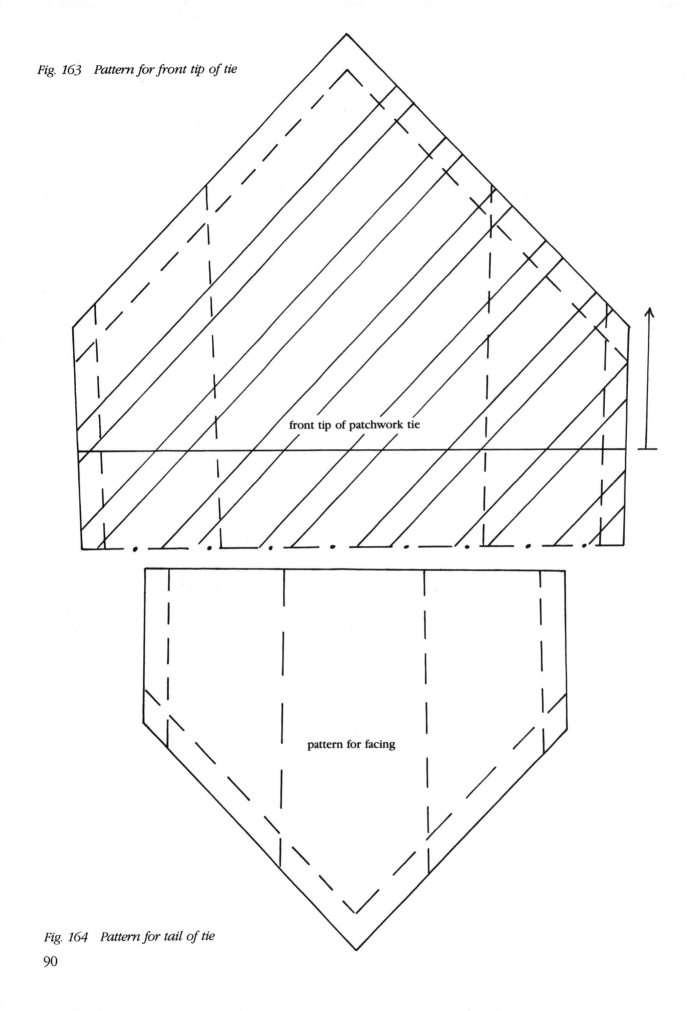

Fig. 163   Pattern for front tip of tie

front tip of patchwork tie

pattern for facing

Fig. 164   Pattern for tail of tie

stitch a strip of contrasting fabric to the first strip. Press the second strip open to the right side, using spray starch to make a crisp fold. Then, stitch a 1″ strip of the main fabric to the contrasting strip; turn open to the right side and press as before. Continue in this manner, adding a contrasting fabric and then a main fabric, ending with a contrasting strip. You can place the contrasting fabrics in a repeating pattern as I have done, or you can add them at random for a less structured result. After the last strip is in place, turn the patchwork over and trim away the excess fabric, even with the edge of the base.

Place the main "tail" fabric on the right side of the tie and pin together. Use the tie as a pattern to cut out the fabric, being sure to cut the angled edge accurately. Stitch the angled edge of the tail piece to the last contrasting strip on the tie as before. Turn to the right side and press. Stitch the tail to the base ¼ inch away from the raw edges.

Cut out 2 facings from the main fabric using the actual-size patterns given here. Fold the long straight edge of each facing ¼ inch to the wrong side; press and stitch in place. With right sides together, stitch the facings to their matching tie ends making a ¼-inch seam. Clip corners, turn right side out and press. Fold the remaining raw edges of the tie ¼ inch to the wrong side and press, using spray starch to make a sharp crease. Then fold the side edges of the tie 1¼ inch to the wrong side. Fold one side over completely; press and baste it in place. Then fold and baste the other side in place. Slip-stitch the upper edge securely to the one beneath it so that the stitches do not show on the right side. Remove basting and press.

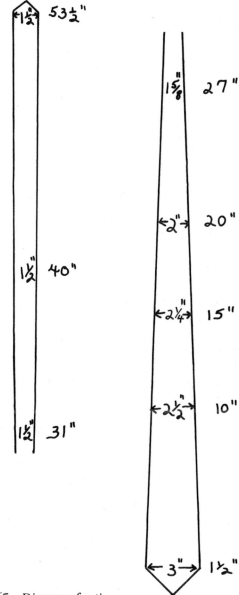

Fig. 165   Diagram for tie

Bookends

See color page K.

Brighten up plain bookshelves with these simple patchwork bookends. They are easy to make and can be adjusted to fit any basic set of plain bookends. You can purchase plastic or metal bookends in an art supply or stationery shop or department store.

Before beginning, review the following sections: *Assembling a Project for Quilting* and *Machine Quilting*.

Easy
Size: To fit your bookends
Requirements
Pieced block: 18 2"-square fabric scraps
Fabric (45" wide): ¼ yard (to match patchwork) for borders and sleeve; muslin or other plain fabric to back the quilting
Batting: 2 large scraps

Instructions: Select one of the 2-inch-square designs from those featured on pages 56–59. Piece 18 squares following the individual diagram. Stitch the squares together in 3 rows with 3 squares in each row. Stitch the rows together, matching seams carefully. Press the finished patchwork.

Measure the face of one of the bookends you wish to cover. Draw these measurements on a sheet of graph paper. Following Fig. 167, measure up ½ inch from the bottom edge and draw a line. Then measure your finished patchwork and draw this measurement (minus ¼ inch all around) on the graph paper, centered between the sides and touching the bottom line. You now have a pattern for the top, bottom and side strips. Cut out these pieces from your matching fabric, being sure to add ¼-inch seam allowances all around each piece. (**Note:** Chances are that the face of your bookends won't be exactly square, but this doesn't matter; the batting will hold out the corners at the top edges.)

Stitch the side strips to each side of the patchwork. Stitch the top and bottom strips in place. Press carefully. Use this piece as a pattern to cut out a piece of batting, muslin and matching fabric for the sleeve. Pin the batting to the wrong side of the patchwork. With right sides facing and raw edges

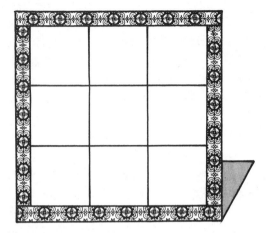

Fig. 166

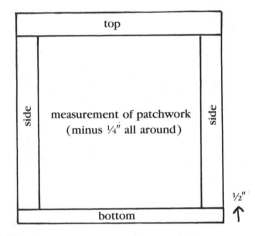

Fig. 167

even, stitch the muslin to the patchwork and batting along the bottom edge only, making a ¼-inch seam. Open out the fabrics and smooth the muslin onto the batting and patchwork. Baste the 3 layers together with all raw edges even. Outline-quilt the patchwork blocks by hand or machine. Stitch ⅛ inch away from the outer raw edges all around.

Fold the raw bottom edge of the fabric sleeve ⅛ inch to the wrong side twice and stitch in place. With right sides facing, and matching the bottom edges, stitch the sleeve to the patchwork at the sides and top edges, making slightly less than a ¼-inch seam. Turn right side out and try it on your plastic or metal bookend for fit. Adjust your seam allowances if the fit is too tight or loose. When satisfied, zigzag-stitch the raw edges on the inside. Repeat for the other bookend.

Shoe Carrier

See color page G.

This is truly a quick and easy project; I completed the entire article in just a few hours. A shoe carrier is unusual yet useful, making it the ideal gift for "the man who has everything." My husband uses it for his golf shoes, but it can be used for carrying shoes for any sporting activity and for keeping shoes away from clean clothes in a suitcase. It is lined in sturdy denim.

Before beginning, read the following sections: *Making a Buttonhole, Machine Quilting,* and *Using a Tube Turner.*

Easy
*Size: 14" × 16", can be adjusted for larger shoes (see **Note** below)*
Requirements
Fabric (45" wide): about ¼ yard fabric (fabric A), plus large scraps of coordinating colors for the corners (fabric B) and pieced blocks
Fabric for side strips (fabric A): 4 strips 2½" × 10½"
*Fabric for top/bottom strips (fabric A): 4 strips 3½" × 10½" (**Note:** If you are making this bag for a very large pair of shoes, increase the width of these strips to 5½" or more; be sure to change the width of the corners to match and adjust the 16½" edge of the denim and the 14½" edge of the batting to correspond with your new measurement.)*
Fabric for corners (fabric B): 8 pieces 2½" × 3½"
*Sturdy denim or poplin fabric in a dark color: 28½" × 16½" (see **Note** above)*
Batting: 14½" × 28½"
Tie: 1¼" × 44" strip of fabric; 44" length of thick cord
Binding: 1½" × 30"

Instructions: Select a 10-inch-square design. Piece 2 blocks as directed in the individual instructions for the designs. Stitch a side strip to each side edge of the blocks. Stitch a corner to each short end of the top/bottom strips matching the 3½-inch edges; stitch to the top and bottom of each block, matching seams carefully. Stitch the 2 patchwork rectangles together along one 16½-inch edge, matching seams. Press carefully.

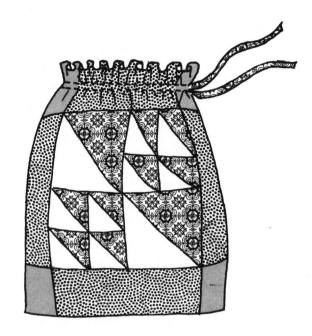

Fig. 168

Next, mark the placement of the buttonholes. With the long edges of the patchwork as the top and bottom, measure down 1¼ inches from the top edge and ¾ inch from each side edge; mark with an **X**. Make a ½-inch buttonhole, centered over each **X**; see *Making a Buttonhole.* The long edge close to the buttonholes will be the top edge of the bag.

Place the batting on the wrong side of the patchwork, matching the bottom and side edges. Baste in place. (**Note:** The batting will not extend to the top of the bag.) Place the patchwork and denim fabrics together with right sides facing, matching all edges. Stitch together along the top edge, making a ¼-inch seam; turn right side out and press along the seam edge only. Carefully pin or baste the patchwork, batting and denim together, matching all edges. To make the casing, stitch 2 parallel lines, ¾ inch and 1¼ inches away from the top edge; the buttonholes

93

should be centered within the casing lines. For decorative purposes, you can add 2 extra lines of stitching, each ¼ to ⅜ inch away from the casing lines, if you wish.

Review *Machine Quilting*; outline-quilt each seam of the patchwork below the casing. Then, stitch ⅛ inch away from the outer edges. Fold the bag in half crosswise with the patchwork sides facing; stitch the side and bottom edges together. Trim off the seam allowance corners at an angle. See *Binding a Project*; bind the raw seam allowance edges as directed, folding the binding under at the beginning and end. Turn the bag right side out, pushing out the corners.

Fold the fabric for the tie in half lengthwise and stitch the long edges together. See *Using a Tube Turner*; turn the strip right side out as directed. Insert the tube turner through the tube and secure the end of the cord in the catch; pull the cord through the tube. Fold the raw fabric edges inside and slip-stitch the ends closed. Insert a small safety pin through one end of the tie, being sure to catch the end of the cord in the pin as well. Insert the safety pin into the casing and ease it along, pulling the tie through the casing. After the tie has been pulled all the way through, even up the ends. Tie knots at the ends, if desired.

Footstool

See color page O.

This footstool will be treasured, particularly if it's made to match a favorite chair. The padded wooden stool is purchased—footstools in a variety of shapes and sizes are available from most arts and crafts shops; you may also find unfinished wooden items of this type at craft and hobby fairs. Or, you might have a worn-out footstool in your attic or garage— why not give it a second life by covering it with patchwork?

Easy
Size: 11½" × 9" × 7" high (although the size of your footstool may vary)
Requirements
Fabric, 45" wide: approximately ¼ to ½ yard of 3 to 4 different fabrics, depending upon the block design that you choose
Footstool, any size
Soft paper (newspaper)
Ruler
Tape
White glue

Instructions: Select a 2-inch square block design from those given on pages 56–59; then determine how many blocks you will need to make as follows. Take some old newspaper and spread it over the pad of your footstool. Draw the outline of the pad as accurately as possible on the newspaper. Remove

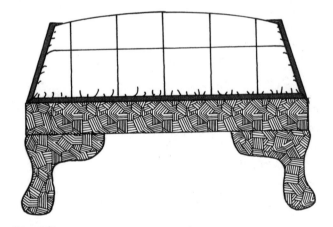

Fig. 169

the newspaper and place on a flat surface. Using a ruler, straighten out your lines and true the corners. Then draw a second rectangle around the first, 2 inches larger all around. Cut out the pattern along the outer lines; you can ignore the inner lines for the moment. Fold and crease the pattern in half crosswise, then lengthwise, to find the exact center. Open up the pattern and draw along the creases. Now, using your ruler and working from the center outward, divide each quarter of the *inner* rectangle into 2-inch squares. Count the number of complete squares and write it down.

In many cases, the 2-inch squares will not fit exactly within the inner rectangle. You have 3 options for the incomplete squares around the edges. **1:** If these squares are smaller than half-size, it would be a waste of effort to make them at all; you can compensate by adding a border in matching fabric all around. Go to the next paragraph. **2:** If the incomplete squares are divided roughly in half, count up the number around the edges (18 for my footstool) and divide that number in half (9 for my footstool). Make this number of squares in addition to your previous total; then cut those exactly in half for the outer edges. Go to the next paragraph. **3:** If the incomplete squares are larger than half, make the entire block; the extra patchwork can be folded underneath the pad. Count up the entire number of blocks around the edges and add that to your previous total.

Make the required number of blocks following the appropriate assembly illustration given with the templates. Sew the blocks together in rows; then sew the rows together, matching seams carefully to complete the pad cover. If you are using option 2, be sure to keep the cut edges of the half-blocks along the outside.

Next, you will need to add a border strip to your patchwork so that it can be secured to the footstool pad. Center the finished patchwork on your newspaper pattern and measure the distance from the raw edges of the patchwork to the outer edge of the paper; this measurement will be the width of your border strips. Cut 2 strips of fabric (to match the background of your patchwork) to this width and the length of each long side of the patchwork; stitch to the patchwork. Then measure the short sides (which now include the border strips); cut 2 more strips to this measurement and the required width. Stitch to the sides of the patchwork. Press carefully.

Place the patchwork on top of the footstool pad. Using pins, secure the fabric to the pad working from the center outward to the edges. Pull the patchwork gently so that it is taut. Continue pulling and stretching the patchwork over the pad until it fits perfectly; you will have to work at the corners to get them as smooth as possible. When you are satisfied, tape the raw edges of the fabric to the bottom of the pad. If you plan to remove the patchwork for cleaning from time to time, you can leave the tape in place; simply cover the messy bottom of the pad with an extra piece of fabric before attaching the pad to the footstool. If you do not plan to remove the cover, glue the raw edges to the bottom of the pad. Cut a piece of fabric to cover the raw edges of the patchwork; then glue the fabric smoothly to the bottom of the pad.

Harlequin Wall Hanging

See color page N.

This handsome wall hanging will enhance any man's office or workplace. It will be fascinating for him to contemplate while he's making decisions, will provide a wonderful focus to his room and may get you some commissions to make more! I have specified the exact colors I used in the instructions below, but you are welcome to change the color scheme as you wish, perhaps in colors to match the decor of the rest of the office.

Before beginning, read the following sections: *Assembling a Project for Quilting, How to Quilt, Binding a Project* and *Hanging a Patchwork Project.*

Easy
Size: About 30" square

Requirements

Fabric, 45" wide: pale blue dotted fabric, 1 yard (to include backing); white, ³⁄₈ yard; black, ³⁄₈ yard; blue, ¹⁄₄ yard; scraps of red, yellow, green and grey
Batting: 30" square
Back: 32¹⁄₂" square pale blue dotted fabric (includes fabric for self-binding)
Sleeve: 3¹⁄₂" × 30" strip pale blue dotted fabric
Number of pieces: 84

A	1 red, 1 blue, 1 yellow, 1 green	M	2 pale blue, 2 pale blue reversed
B	12 black	N	2 blue strips 1¹⁄₄" × 22¹⁄₄"
C	4 white	O	2 blue strips 1¹⁄₄" × 24¹⁄₄"
D	4 blue	P	4 white strips 1³⁄₄" × 24¹⁄₄"
E	4 pale blue		
F	4 white	Q	4 grey squares 1³⁄₄" × 1³⁄₄"
G	4 black		
H	4 pale blue	R	4 black strips 2¹⁄₂" × 27¹⁄₄"
J	4 white, 4 white reversed		
K	4 grey, 2 red, 2 blue, 2 yellow, 2 green		
L	2 pale blue, 2 pale blue reversed		

Fig. 170

Instructions: Following the assembly diagrams (Fig. 171 and Fig. 172), assemble the wall hanging from the middle outward. First, sew the four A pieces together. Next, sew a B to each A-A edge. Sew a C to each B-B edge. Sew a D to each C-C edge. Sew an E to each D-D edge. Next, sew the F and G pieces around the center in a circular manner following Figs. 173 and 174. First, sew an F to E, ending your stitching halfway across the F piece as shown in Fig. 173. Stitch a G to the straight edge formed by F-E-E; then sew an F to the adjacent G-E seam. Continue around the patchwork in this manner until you reach the last G (Fig. 173). Stitch the last G to E-E-F; then stitch the remaining portion of the first F to E-G (Fig. 174).

Next, sew a B to adjacent edges of a red, blue, yellow and green K square, making a triangle. Stitch the B-B edge of each triangle to each F-G seam. Next, assemble the 4 H-J-K triangles. Stitch an H to the short edge of 4 J's, matching the dots. Stitch a grey K to each of the remaining 4 J's; then stitch J-K to H-J to complete each triangle. Following the assembly diagram, stitch an L and then an M to each of

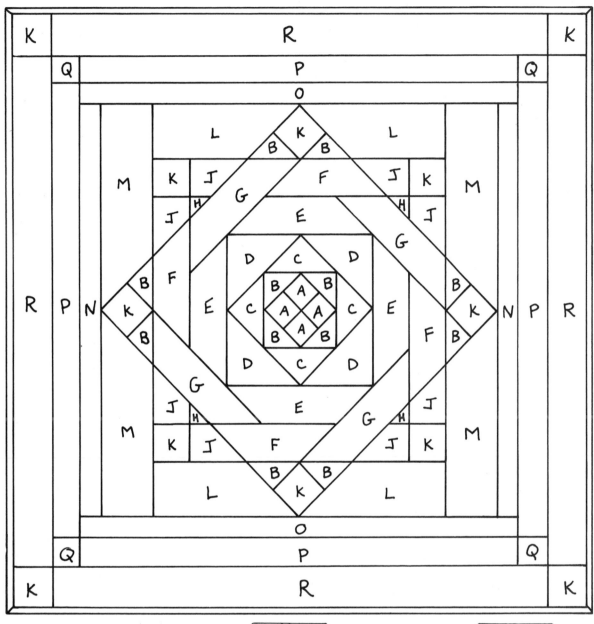

Fig. 171

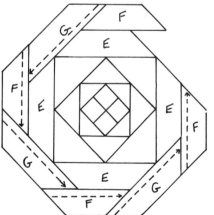

Fig. 172   Stitch F to E, ending stitching halfway across F.

Fig. 173   Stitch G to F-E-E, then stitch F to G-E. Continue around the patchwork in this manner.

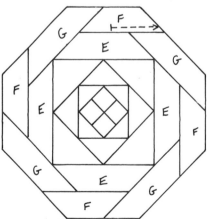

Fig. 174   Stitch the last G to E-E-F, then stitch the remaining portion of the first F to E-G.

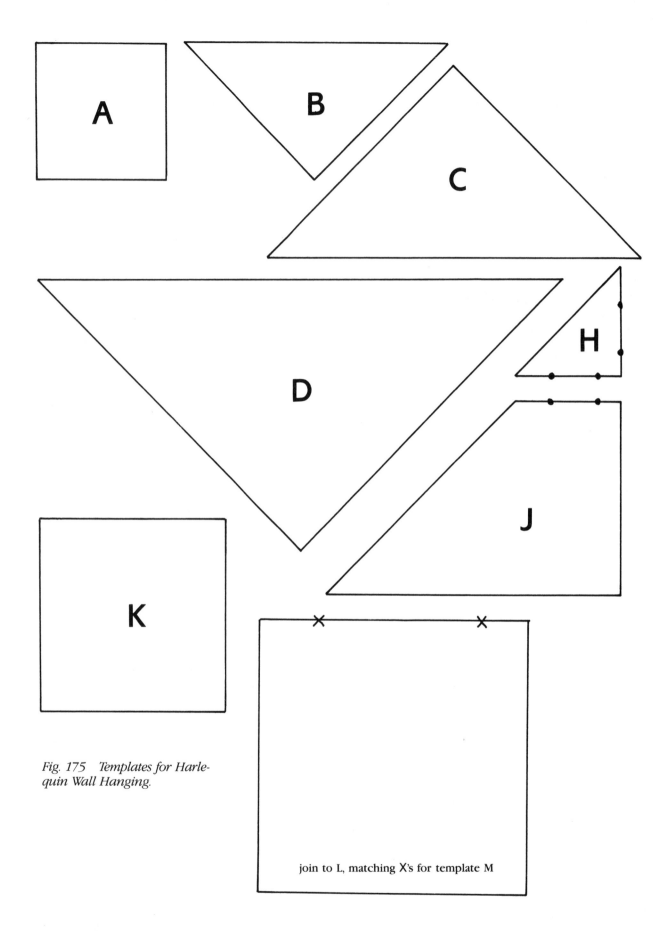

Fig. 175 *Templates for Harle-quin Wall Hanging.*

join to L, matching X's for template M

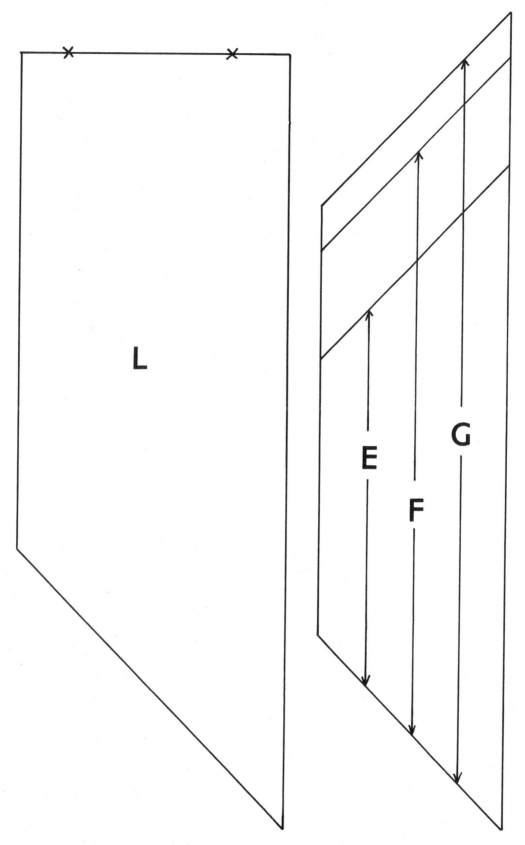

*Fig. 176   Templates for Harle-
quin Wall Hanging, continued*

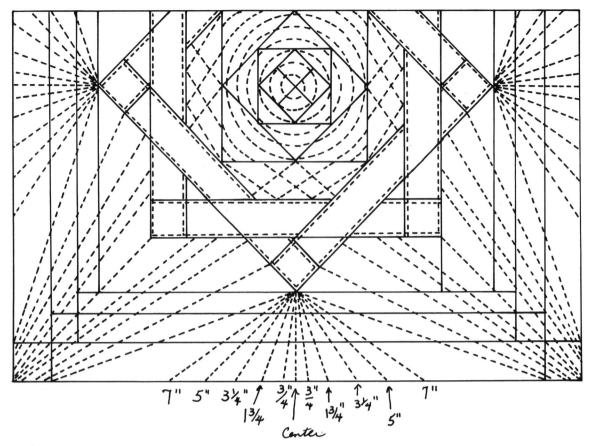

7" 5" 3¼" ↑ ¾" ¾" ↑ ↑ ↑ 7"
          1¾"   1¾" 3¼"
              ↑   5"
           Center

*Fig. 177 Partial quilting pattern
for Harlequin Wall Hanging*

these triangles to make the 4 large corner triangles. Stitch each corner triangle in place, matching seams very carefully to create the illusion of the intertwined strips.

Finally, add the outer borders. Sew an N to each side of the patchwork. Sew an O to the top and bottom edges. Sew a P to each side edge. Sew a Q to each short end of the remaining 2 P's; sew Q-P-Q to the top and bottom edges of the patchwork. Sew an R to each side edge. Sew a K to each short end of the remaining 2 R's; sew K-R-K to the top and bottom edges of the patchwork to finish. Press very carefully.

See *Assembling a Project for Quilting*; assemble the patchwork, batting and back as directed, placing the batting and patchwork in the exact middle of the back. Quilt the wall hanging by hand or machine following the partial quilting diagram (Fig. 177). You do not need to quilt the project as thoroughly as I have; simple outline quilting of each of the pieces will suffice if you are short on time. See the instructions for self-binding in *Binding a Project*; bind the edges of the wall hanging as directed, mitring the corners. Make and attach a sleeve to the back of the wall hanging as directed in *Hanging a Patchwork Project*. Be sure to sign and date the back or front of your masterpiece!

TREASURES FOR THE HOME

Home Sweet Home Wall Hanging *See color page J.*

What a perfect gift for someone who has just moved house and has a lot of bare walls to decorate! Choose fabrics in the colors of the new home for the central block design; then use your imagination for the surrounding houses. Select a fabric that will blend in with the new home's color scheme for the back and corners of the wall hanging.

Before beginning, review the following sections: *Assembling a Project for Quilting, Binding a Project* and *Hanging a Project.*

Easy
Finished Size: 36" × 36" octagon
Requirements
Pieced blocks: 5 10" square—¼ yard each of 8–10 fabrics
Sashing: 18 short sashes 1½" × 10½"; 2 long sashes 1½" × 12½"—¼ yard light fabric
Accent squares: 16 1½" squares—⅛ yard bright fabric
Corners and back: 4 right-angle triangles 12½" × 12½" × 17⅝" (cut from each corner of yardage); use remaining piece of yardage for the back—1¼ yards dark fabric
Batting: 36½" × 36½" octagon
Binding: self-binding
Sleeves: 1 3" × 11" (top) and 1 3" × 35" (lower)—coordinating fabric
Flat, lightweight strips of wood for hanging: 1 2" × 10" and 1 2" × 34"

Instructions: Select five 10-inch-square house designs from those featured in Chapter 2; piece each one as directed in the individual instructions. (**Note:** Because there are many different fabrics in

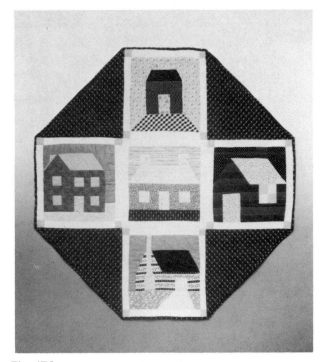

Fig. 178

each block, the fabric used for the sky has simply been labelled "sky" in the fabric list and instructions. Choose whatever blue shade or print that you deem most suitable for each design. Also, in some cases, "grass" and "gravel" are also listed as fabric colors; again, choose a suitable fabric.)

After the blocks have been completed, sew a short sash to each side edge of each block. Sew the accent squares to each edge of the remaining short sashes. Arrange the blocks as shown in Fig. 178. When you are satisfied with your arrangement, sew the long sashes to the top and bottom edges of the central block. Sew the pieced sashes to the top and

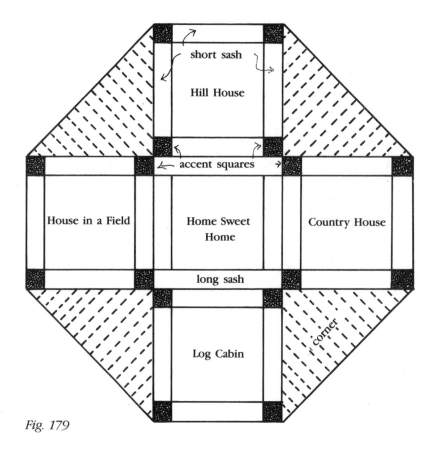

short sash

Hill House

accent squares

House in a Field   Home Sweet Home   Country House

long sash

Log Cabin

corner

Fig. 179

bottom edges of the remaining blocks. Following Fig. 179, arrange the blocks and corner pieces on a flat surface; separate into 3 horizontal rows. Sew the pieces in each row together. Then, matching all seams carefully, pin and stitch the 3 rows together to complete the top.

For the back, place the quilt top over the octagon-shaped piece previously cut, keeping the grain straight. Trim the back to ½" away from the edge of the top.

See *Assembling a Project for Quilting*; assemble the wall hanging as directed. Quilt the blocks following the individual instructions. Quilt the corners with parallel lines of diagonal stitches following Fig. 179. Review *Binding a Project*; self-bind the project as directed, mitring the corners.

See *Hanging a Patchwork Project*. Sew the top sleeve to the upper back edge of the wall hanging; this is the sleeve that is used to actually hang the project. Stitch the lower sleeve to the upper edge of the widest part of the octagon. The lower sleeve is used to hold the side edges of the wall hanging straight out. Insert the lightweight flat wooden strips through the appropriate sleeves.

As a variation, use this project as a table covering. Select a design for the central block that does not have a definite top or bottom. Then arrange 4 house blocks around the central square, so that the top edge of each house is sewn to the central square. Do not attach sleeves to the back.

Doorstop

See color page C.

This easy-to-make doorstop will be a welcome gift for someone who is moving to another house or redecorating their home. Make the doorstop in colors to match the room; you can even make a coordinating cushion—see the House Cushion project. For the best effect, select a design that has a central focus, such as Swing Music (seen in the example in the Color Section) rather than one that creates a picture such as Regatta.

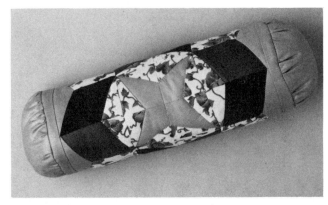

Fig. 180

Before beginning, review the following sections: *Assembling a Project for Quilting* and *Machine Quilting.*

Easy
Size: About 14" long × 4" high
Requirements
Pieced block: 1 10" square—fabric scraps
Fabric (45" wide): ⅛ yard or large scrap to match patchwork for borders and ends; muslin or other plain fabric to back the quilting
Batting: 1 12" × 13" piece
Sand in 5 small plastic bags
Polyester fibrefill

Instructions: Select one of the 10-inch-square designs from those featured on pages 56–59. Piece one square following the individual instructions. From matching fabric, cut 2 side strips, each 10½" × 1" and one bottom strip 2½" × 11". Stitch the side strips to opposite sides of the block. Stitch the bottom strip to one of the remaining raw edges of the block (Fig. 181). Following the instructions for *Assembling a Project for Quilting*, assemble the patchwork with the batting and muslin; quilt by machine following the individual instructions for the block; do not quilt along the bottom or side strips. Machine-stitch ⅛ inch away from the raw edges all around. Stitch the remaining raw edge of the block to the long raw edge of the bottom strip, creating a tube of fabric; leave a 3-inch opening in this seam for stuffing. Do not turn the fabric tube right side out yet.

Cut two 5½"-diameter circles from matching fabric. Machine-baste ¼ inch away from the raw edges all around. Pin to the ends of the fabric tube, gather-

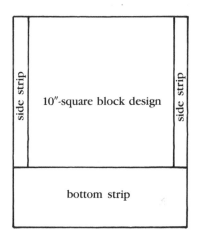

side strip   10"-square block design   side strip

bottom strip

Fig. 181

ing the circles to fit evenly all around. Stitch a circle to each end of the tube. Turn the tube right side out through the opening.

Carefully stuff the ends of the tube with fibrefill. Insert a sandbag into the tube at each end, and stuff with more fibrefill to hold the bags in place. (**Note:** As you are adding the sandbags, make sure that they weight the doorstop along the bottom strip and not at the top!) Add 2 more bags and repeat. Add one more bag to the middle; then continue stuffing until the tube is round and plump. Fold the raw edges at the opening inside and slip-stitch the opening closed. Place the doorstop on the floor just in front of the open door.

House Cushion

See color page C.

A cushion provides a wonderful accent to any room, and is always a welcome gift. This one is especially quick to make, so if you have forgotten someone's birthday or anniversary, spend an afternoon creating this project and your problem will be solved.

Before beginning, review the following sections: *Assembling a Project for Quilting, Machine Quilting* and *Ruffle.*

Easy
Finished size: 13" square, excluding ruffle

Requirements

Pieced block: 1 10" square—fabric scraps
Border: 4 1½" × 10½" strips—⅛ yard coordinating fabric; 4 accent squares 1½" × 1½"—fabric scrap in contrasting color (use a small amount of this fabric in the block design)
Muslin or neutral fabric for backing (if quilting): 13½" square
Batting (if quilting): 13½" square
Ruffle: 4 3½" × 28"—½ yard fabric (scraps of this can be used to construct the block design)
Back: 2 7¼" × 13½" fabric pieces
Zipper: 1 12" long
Pillow form: 1 14" square

Instructions: Select a 10-inch-square-block design. Piece the block as directed in the individual instructions. Stitch a border strip to each side of the pieced block. Stitch an accent square to each end of the remaining 2 border strips. Stitch the pieced border strips to the top and bottom edges of the pieced block, matching seams carefully.

If you wish to quilt the design, see *Assembling a Project for Quilting.* Assemble the patchwork, batting and backing as directed; quilt the pillow front following the individual instructions for the block and your own design for the border. To save time, you may wish to machine-quilt the design; see *Machine Quilting.*

Next, make the ruffle; see *Ruffle.* With right sides facing, stitch the short ends of the ruffle strips to each other. (Fig. 19), forming a continuous circle of fabric. Fold the fabric in half lengthwise with wrong

Fig. 182

sides facing and press; machine-baste ¼ inch away from the raw edges all around (Fig. 20). Gently pull the basting stitches, gathering the ruffle to approximately fit the edges of the pillow front (Fig. 21). With raw edges even, pin the ruffle to the right side of the pillow front so that a seam is located at each corner. Adjust the gathers evenly to fit, allowing extra gathers or making a pleat at each of the corners (Fig. 22). Stitch the ruffle to the pillow front.

Next, make the pillow back. Pin the 2 back pieces together at the long edges; mark off the 12-inch zipper length, centered evenly between the top and bottom. With right sides facing, stitch the long edges together, making a ½-inch seam. Sew with small stitches above and below the zipper markings; change to a basting stitch within the marked zipper section. Press the seam open. Sew the zipper in place following the manufacturer's instructions.

Pin the back to the front with right sides facing, raw edges even and the ruffle sandwiched in between. Stitch together ¼ inch from the edges all around. Clip off each of the 4 corners at an angle; then turn right side out. Insert the pillow form through the zipper opening.

Maple Leaf Quilt

See color page F

It was lying at the bottom of a pile of quilts, neatly folded and with a small tag that read: "Hand-pieced in Kansas, 1930s." I carefully unfolded the quilt top and immediately fell in love with it. It spoke to me in a way that many finished quilts do not. As we examined the quilt top in that cramped antiques shop in California, I felt an affinity with the woman who pieced her Maple Leaf creation almost 60 years ago. The price was very reasonable and I bought it within moments. After talking with the shopkeeper for a while, I was going to leave when she stopped me. "I've had that quilt top for a long time," she said, "and I wasn't sure whether I really wanted to sell it. But I'm glad it was bought by a quilter who appreciates it the way you obviously do."

Later, I spread the quilt top out on the floor of my brother and sister-in-law's living room, and we all knelt down to examine my treasure. There were many exclamations of wonder, such as "Look at this fabric; do you suppose it's flour sacking?" and "Look how she pieced this area—that plaid triangle is made of 3 different sections, and it looks like an uncut fabric!" and "I wonder why she used these two shades of yellow—did she run out of fabric? Then, if so, why does she have another piece of the same yellow here?" As we studied the quilt, we suddenly realized that even though this unknown woman was short of fabric, having to piece many of the squares and triangles comprising the maple leaf pattern, she still managed to arrange the blocks in a definite order—a red leaf in the center surrounded by green leaves and more red leaves; a blue leaf in each corner, and plaids, yellows and mauves in an ordered arrangement on the rest of the top. She obviously had enough solid blue-and-white printed fabric for the sashing, which, because of its unusual width, forms a striking part of the overall design.

I returned home to London and began preparing the top for quilting so that I could include the finished project in this book. There were many frayed edges and hanging threads and it took me over 8 hours to clean up the back of the quilt to my satisfaction. But as I worked, I found more secrets: tiny corners of triangles and squares that were skilfully

Fig. 183

pieced with a virtually invisible seam on the right side; a leaf that seems to have deliberately mismatched fabrics; the block that has been pieced to absolute perfection, with the printed stripes matching so well that the leaf looks as if it hasn't been pieced at all. Obviously this woman had talent. Her firm, sure stitches had not unravelled at all, her corners matched, and her work lay absolutely flat. I hoped that what I was about to do would have met her approval had she been around to express it.

I'm writing this story in between quilting sessions. As I quilt, I wonder about this woman. Is she still alive or did she die before she could finish her work? How could she part with her quilt top, which was so lovingly pieced—was she forced to sell or barter it in order to feed her family? This is a definite possibility since the quilt was pieced during the Depression. This would also explain why it was unfinished—in those days, the batting and backing were very expensive parts of the quilt; perhaps she couldn't afford to finish it. Or maybe she never married and had no reason to finish her quilt top. So many possibilities, so many questions. As I sit and quilt and wonder, I realize that the experience of finishing an antique quilt is entirely different from finishing a modern one. And I'm enjoying getting to

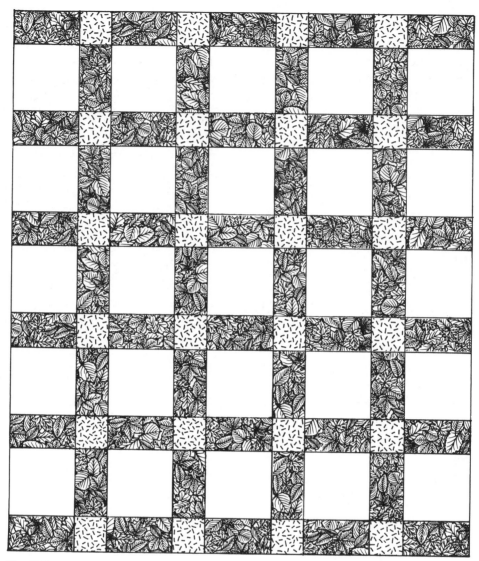

Fig. 184

know this woman from Kansas while I complete her work.

Before beginning, review the following sections: *Assembling a Project for Quilting, Making Templates, How to Quilt*, and *Binding a Project*.

Easy
Finished size: 70" × 80"
Requirements
Pieced blocks: 25 10" squares—large scraps of closely woven cotton fabric in a variety of colors (fabric amounts will vary according to the block design chosen and how many times you repeat a fabric in the quilt top, but you'll need an average of 1½ yards each of 5–6 different fabrics)

*Sashing: 30 5½" × 10½" pieces dark fabric—1¼ yards; see **Note** under "Back"; 24 5½" squares light fabric—½ yard*
*Back: 2 36" × 80½"—5 yards fabric to match sashing. **Note:** 5½ yards will be enough for both the back and the dark sashing.*
Batting: 71" × 81"
Binding: strip 1" × 304" cut on straight grain of fabric—¼ yard fabric to contrast with sashing

Instructions: For the quilt top, select a 10-inch-square design. Piece 25 blocks following the individual instructions. The block used for the quilt in the photograph is called Maple Leaf; patterns and instructions are on page 42. (**Note:** If you wish, you can choose 25 different block designs and make a sampler-style quilt.) Arrange the blocks on a flat surface in 5 rows with 5 blocks in each row. When you are satisfied with the arrangement, sew a dark sash between each block following Fig. 183; do not sew a sash to the outer edges of the end blocks. Next, construct 6 sashing strips by sewing the short edge of a dark sash to each light sashing square; in each strip, there will be 5 dark sashes separated by 4 light squares. Finally, sew the pieced sashing strips to each side of the block/sashing strips, matching all seams. Press the quilt top very carefully.

For the back, stitch the long edges of the fabric pieces together, making a ½" seam. Press the seam allowance to one side.

See *Assembling a Project for Quilting*. Assemble the quilt top as directed, basting the layers together very well. Quilt the blocks following the individual instructions, working from the central block outward. See *Making Templates*. Construct a sturdy template for each of the quilting designs on the following pages, or create your own quilting patterns to fit into the sashing. Using a light marking pencil, trace around the templates to transfer 2 leaf patterns to each dark sash; arrange the leaves so that they are tumbling and turning in different directions and in different combinations on each piece. Using a hard lead pencil, transfer a "Fruit of Maple" (mapleseed) pattern to each light sashing square, turning the fruit in different directions on each square. Quilt the designs along the marked outlines.

Trim the outer edges of the quilt so that they are even. Review *Binding a Quilt* for instructions on making and attaching the binding. Bind the quilt all around, mitring the corners.

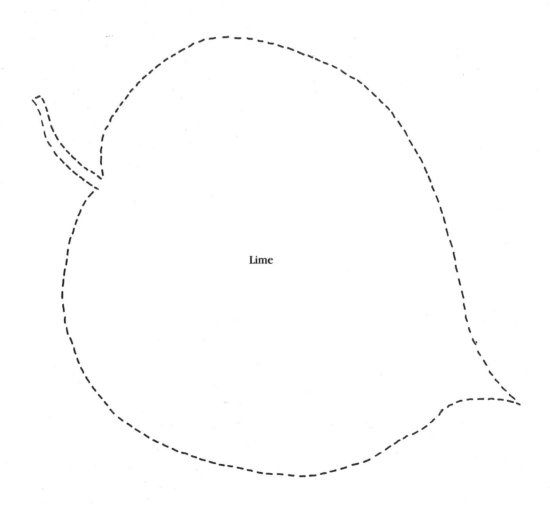

Lime

*Fig. 185 Quilting pattern for
Maple Leaf Quilt*

Oak

Tulip

Fruit of Maple

Fig. 186 Quilting patterns for
Maple Leaf Quilt, continued

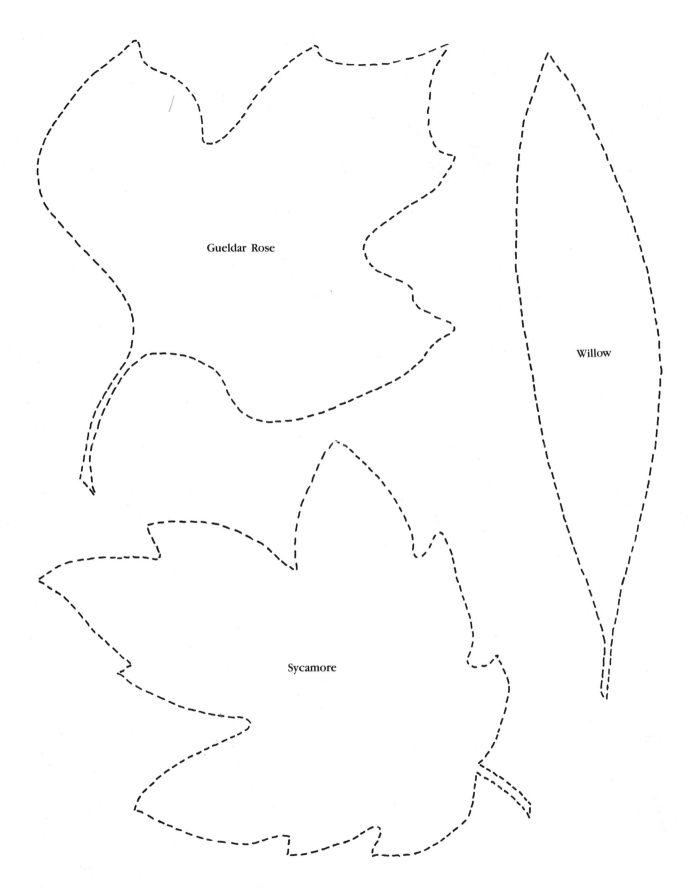

Gueldar Rose

Willow

Sycamore

Fig. 187   Quilting patterns for
Maple Leaf Quilt, continued

CHRISTMAS KEEPSAKES

Christmas Clown

See color page A.

Easy
Finished Size: About 12" tall
Requirements
Fabric: scraps in bright colors in a wide variety of solids and prints; white or ecru fabric scrap
Felt: red, black and yellow scraps
Embroidery floss: blue, red, black and green
Novelty buttons, each ⅜-inch diameter: 4
Medium-weight string or crochet cotton: 1 yard
Polyester fibrefill stuffing
Embroidery needle
Large-eyed needle with a sharp point
Stiff cardboard or plastic for template
Compass

Fig. 188

Instructions: To make the yo-yo's for the arms and legs, cut a 5-inch-diameter circle template from heavy cardboard or plastic. Use the template to mark and cut out 12 circles for each arm and 16 for each leg from your fabric scraps, for a total of 56 circles. Securely knot the end of a length of neutral sewing thread, such as ecru or grey, and take 3 backstitches in the same place along the edge of the first circle before beginning. Work a running stitch ⅛ inch away from the edge of the first circle on the right side of the fabric (Fig. 189). Pull the thread, gathering the fabric edges into a tight circle (Fig. 190). Knot the end of the thread, again work 3 backstitches in the same place, and then cut off the excess thread. Gently flatten the circle with the gathered raw edges centered on one side (Fig. 191). Repeat for the rest of the circles.

Trace the full-size patterns for the body, glove and boot; complete the half-pattern for the body. Mark 2 bodies on the white or ecru fabric, transferring the facial features onto one piece only. Using 2 strands of embroidery floss in the needle, embroider blue eyes in star stitch, red nose and mouth in satin stitch, and black eyebrows in outline stitch. Gently press the finished embroidery on the wrong side; then cut out the body pieces, being sure to add ¼ inch around the edges for the seam allowance.

With right sides facing and raw edges even, stitch the body pieces together leaving the bottom edge open. Clip the seam allowances at the curves; then turn right side out. Sew the novelty buttons to the embroidered body piece at the positions indicated by the circles. For the arms and legs, cut 2 lengths of

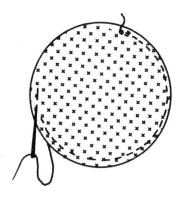

Fig. 189 Knot the end of a length of thread, then work three backstitches on the right side of the circle fabric. Sew a running stitch ⅛-inch from the edge all around.

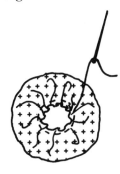

Fig. 190 Pull the thread, gathering the edges of the fabric into a tight circle.

Fig. 191 Flatten the circle with the gathered edges centered on one side.

crochet cotton or string, one 15 inches long for the arms and one 20 inches long for the legs. Thread each end of the arm string into a large-eyed needle. From inside the body, bring out the needle and string at the position indicated by an asterisk (*), pulling until about 5 inches of string extends from the body; repeat on the other side of the body with the other needle and remaining length of string. Loop the leg string around the arm string inside the body to secure it; then stuff the body until plump, allowing the leg strings to hang evenly out of the

opening at the bottom of the body. Turn the raw edges at the opening ¼ inch to the inside and pin together so that the leg strings emerge at the positions marked with dots. Slip-stitch the bottom edges of the body together, securing the leg strings in the seam at the appropriate positions.

Divide your yo-yo's into 2 groups of 12 for the arms and 2 groups of 16 for the legs, being sure to mix the colors evenly throughout each group. Each of the arm strings should still be threaded onto a large-eyed needle. Insert the point of one needle through the center of the ungathered (flat) side of the first yo-yo. After this, insert the needle through the gathered center of each of the remaining 11 yo-yo's. Knot the end of the string securely, cutting away any excess string. Repeat for the other arm. Thread the large-eyed needles with the leg strings and thread the yo-yo's onto the leg strings in the same manner as the arms, using 16 yo-yo's for each.

Using the patterns, cut 4 gloves from the red felt and 4 boots from the black felt. Stitch 2 matching pairs of gloves and boots together around the curved edges, stitching about ⅛ inch away from the edges of the felt. Leave the straight edges open. Stuff each until plump. Stitch the straight edges of the gloves and boots to the last yo-yo at the ends of the arms and legs respectively, hiding the knots from the strings inside.

To attach the hair, use 6 strands of green embroidery floss in the needle. Make loopy stitches all around the top and back of the head working the loops quite close together. Cut into the loops if desired to create strands. To make a beret, cut a red circle of fabric using your template. Prepare the circle as if making a yo-yo, but pull the thread just tight enough so that it fits around the clown's head; knot the end of the thread. Fold the raw fabric edges inside, and slip-stitch the beret to the clown's head all around.

Using the pattern, cut one red and one yellow collar from felt; do not add seam allowances. Clip into one collar along the solid line and the other along the dash line. Place around the clown's neck with the clips at the back. Slip-stitch the cut edges together.

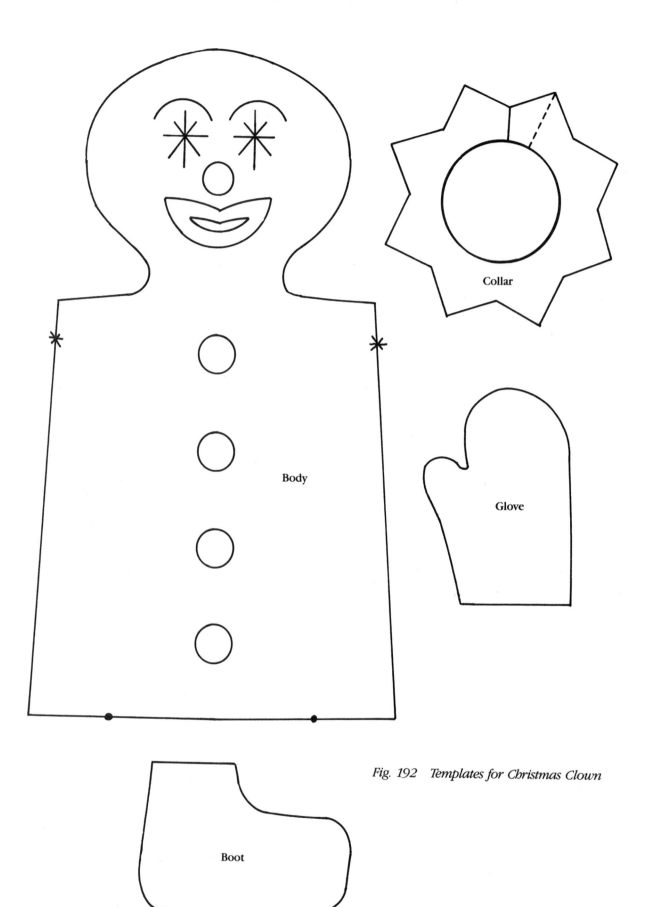

Body

Collar

Glove

Boot

Fig. 192   Templates for Christmas Clown

Holiday Shawl

See color page E.

Snuggle into this gorgeous shawl at Christmas or any other time of the year. You'll feel warm, wonderful and extremely pampered with this around your shoulders. And think of what an impressive Christmas or birthday gift a patchwork shawl will make! Depending upon the patchwork pattern you choose and how much quilting you decide to do, you can easily complete the project in only a few hours.

Before beginning, review the following sections: *Assembling a Project for Quilting* and *Binding a Project.*

Easy
Size: 56" wide × 40" deep
Requirements
Fabric: 45" wide: 1½ yards main color (for patchwork, triangles, and the back); ½ yard of highly contrasting fabric (for patchwork and binding); ¼ yard each of third or fourth colors for the patchwork (only if required for the pattern you have chosen)
Batting: 41" × 41" × 57" triangle
Triangles: 4 using pattern (place on fold of fabric)—main color
Back: 41" × 41" × 57" triangle—main color
Binding: 2" × 139"—contrasting color

Instructions: Select a 10-inch-square design; piece 6 blocks following the individual instructions. Following the assembly diagram (Fig. 194), arrange the patchwork blocks and triangles on a flat surface. Separate the pieces into vertical rows; stitch together in rows. Next, stitch the rows together, matching seams carefully, to complete the large triangular shape. Press carefully, being careful not to stretch the long edge if the pieces have been cut on the bias.

See *Assembling a Project for Quilting*; assemble the shawl, batting and back as directed. Hand- or machine-quilt the patchwork blocks following the individual instructions. If you have empty spaces around your patchwork pieces, such as those between the Feathery Star blocks in the photograph, transfer a single star or an arrangement of several stars to the empty spaces; quilt the designs by hand

Fig. 193

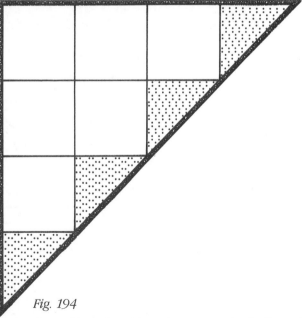

Fig. 194

or machine. Transfer either the star or the holly and bow design to each of the triangles; quilt the designs. Bind the shawl as directed in *Binding a Project*, mitring the corners.

113

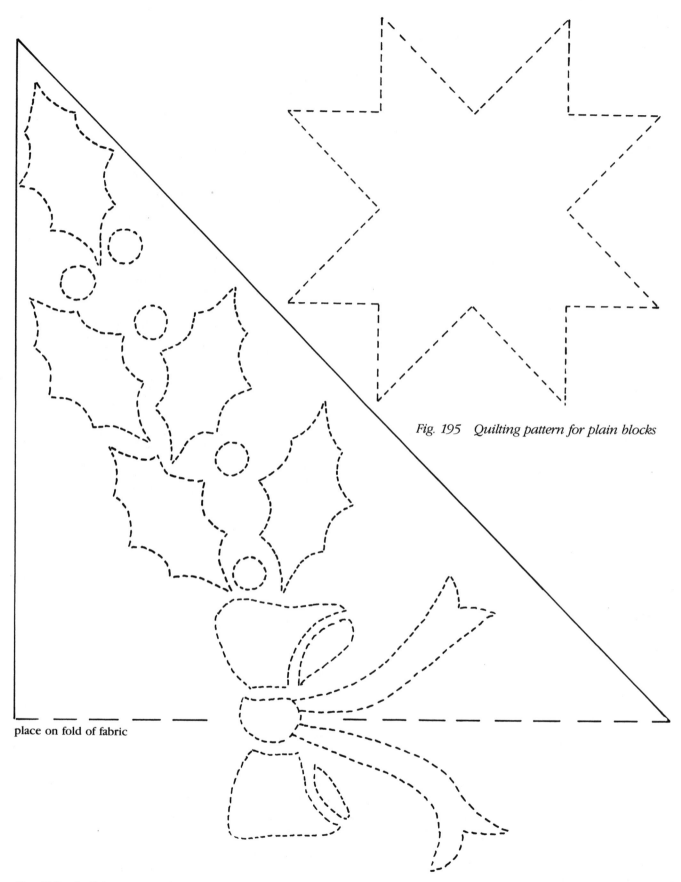

Fig. 195 Quilting pattern for plain blocks

place on fold of fabric

Fig. 196 Quilting pattern for triangular blocks

Yuletide Stocking

See color page D.

This luscious concoction of lace, ribbons and brightly colored fabrics will enchant your favorite little boy or girl at Christmastime. It is very quick and easy to make and will enable you to use up all those scraps of ribbon or lace that you have been saving.

Before beginning, review the following sections: *Rotary Cutting, Quilt-As-You-Go, Binding a Project* and *Loops & Ties.*

Easy
Finished size: About 14" long × 10" wide at the foot

Requirements

Stocking front: ³⁄₈ yard muslin or other neutral cotton fabric; scraps of fabric in Christmas colors; scraps of ³⁄₈"-wide ribbon in Christmas colors; scraps of ¹⁄₂" and ³⁄₄"-wide lace trim
Stocking back: ³⁄₈ yard brightly colored Christmas fabric
Cuff: 1¹⁄₂" to 2"-wide embroidered cotton trim—³⁄₈ yard
Double-fold bias seam binding: 1 package red or green (a little more than 1 yard is required, if you already have an opened package)

Instructions: Trace the full-size pattern for the foot of the stocking; see Fig. 198. Draw a 6½" × 7½" rectangle on a sheet of paper, cut it out and tape it to the top of the foot pattern. Use this complete pattern to cut one stocking from muslin. For the back, use the pattern in reverse to cut one stocking from Christmas fabric; set the back aside for now.

Cut your fabric scraps into strips. The strips need not be even; in fact, it is better if they are slightly uneven—this will add interest and a feeling of movement to your finished project. Cut the strips with scissors, or cut several strips at one time following the instructions for *Rotary Cutting.* Arrange the strips on top of the muslin stocking so as to get the best possible mix of pattern and colors. When you are satisfied with your arrangement, begin sewing the strips to the muslin stocking following the instructions for *Quilt-As-You-Go;* you do not need to

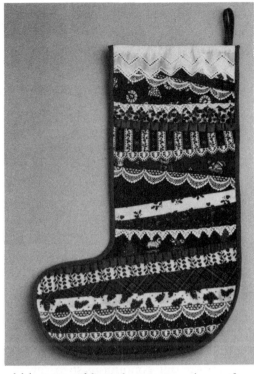

Fig. 197

add batting, although you may do so if you wish to achieve a more sculptured effect.

Begin at the bottom edge by placing your first strip right side up on the right side of the muslin so that the bottom edges match; pin or baste the strip in place. Place the next strip over the first strip with right sides facing and raw edges approximately matching; stitch in place along the top edge. Fold the second strip up and press. Continue adding fabric strips to the stocking in this manner until all the muslin is covered. If you wish to add lace to one of the fabric strips, pin the lace on top of the appropriate strip, with the top edge of the lace slightly below the raw edge of the strip; baste in place. Place the next strip on top of the lace, with right sides facing; stitch together securing the lace in the seam, fold the new strip up and press. You can add ribbon in the same way as the lace; for a 3-dimensional effect, pleat the ribbon as shown in the color photograph. When the stocking is finished, press carefully; then turn wrong-side-up. Trim away the uneven edges of the strips so that they are even with the edge of the muslin. Topstitch ⅛ inch away from the edge of the stocking front all around.

Fig. 198   Template for foot of Christmas stocking

Attach the "cuff" to the stocking front and back as follows: Pin the embroidered cotton trim to the short top edge of each stocking piece with the right side of the trim facing the wrong side of the stocking; stitch in place making a ¼-inch seam. Press the seam allowance towards the stocking and zigzag-stitch in place. Press the cuff down towards the right side of the stocking.

Next, assemble the stocking. With wrong sides facing and raw edges even, stitch the front to the back making a ⅛-inch seam; catch the raw side edges of the cuffs into your stitching. Finish the raw edges of the stocking with double-fold bias seam binding. Unfold one side of the binding, and with right sides facing and raw edges even, stitch to the stocking front in one continuous strip, sewing along the fold line of the binding; start at the top back edge and end at the top front; leave about ¼-inch excess binding at each end. Wrap the binding over the raw edges of the stocking, easing around the curved areas, and slip-stitch to the back with matching thread. You may wish to trim the raw edges of the stocking ever so slightly at the curves for ease in folding the binding to the back. Fold the raw ends of the binding under twice and slip-stitch inside the stocking. See *Loops & Ties*. Make a 3-inch loop with a scrap of binding and slip-stitch the ends inside the stocking at the top back edge.

Continue lines upwards for 7½"

Christmas Tree Ornaments

See color page D.

Patchwork ornaments add such a charming touch to a Christmas tree. They're so quick to make that you can complete several in an afternoon (and have lots of fun while you're doing it!). You can select any of the shapes given here, or choose from the 2-inch-square designs on pages 56–59.

You can choose from 2 styles of ornaments: flat or stuffed. The flat ornaments can be made with batting for a puffy effect, if you wish. Alternatively, the ornaments can be stuffed with fibrefill, potpourri, or even pine needles. Both styles are shown in the Color Section and in the illustrations on these pages.

Variation: For quick bazaar-type items, you can make these designs into sachets or pincushions by using non-Christmas fabrics and eliminating the hanging loops.

Before beginning, review the following sections: *Assembling a Project for Quilting, Quilt-As-You-Go, Binding a Project*, and *Loops & Ties*.

Fig. 199

Easy
Size: From 2″ square to 3½″ diameter

Requirements
Fabric scraps in a variety of Christmas colors; scraps of ¼″, ½″ and ¾″-wide lace trim; scraps of bias binding in Christmas colors
For the loops: bias binding or ribbon 6″–7″ length for each ornament
Batting (optional) for a flat ornament; or fibrefill, potpourri or pine needles for a stuffed ornament

Instructions: To make an ornament, select a design and piece as directed in the individual instructions. Using the pieced front as a pattern, cut the back from a scrap of matching fabric. Decide whether you'd like a flat or stuffed ornament; then select one of the 3 finishing styles given below: plain, lace or bound. You will need approximately ⅜ yard of lace or ½ yard of bias binding for the lace or bound finishes. (**Note**: You can add lace only to the stuffed ornaments.)

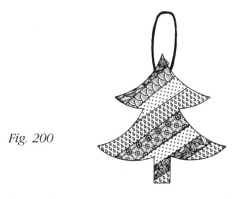

Fig. 200

Flat, plain ornaments: See Fig. 200. With right sides facing and raw edges even, stitch the ornament front to the back, leaving a 1½″ opening along one edge. (**Note:** For the Christmas tree, I left the whole trunk area unstitched and then turned those edges inside by hand later. I do not recommend this finish for the Candy Cane; that should be made by the flat, bound method.) Turn the ornament right side out through the opening, pushing out any points or corners. Fold the raw edges at the opening inside and slip-stitch closed. Make a loop or tie from ribbon and slip-stitch to the top or back of the ornament.

Fig. 201

Fig. 203

Flat, bound ornaments: See Fig. 201. If you wish to add batting, use the pieced front as a pattern to cut out one piece of batting. Assemble the 3 layers following the instructions for *Assembling a Project for Quilting*. Hand- or machine-quilt the ornament as desired. I quilted "in the ditch" (very close to the seam line) to accentuate the patchwork pieces. When the quilting is finished (or if you decide not to quilt at all), machine-stitch ⅛″ away from the raw edges all around. Trim the edges evenly; then bind the ornament following the instructions for *Binding a Project*. If you can, continue the binding up along one side edge for about 5″ to make the loop; stitch the end of the binding to the back of the ornament to finish the loop. Otherwise, make a separate loop; see *Loops & Ties*.

Stuffed lacy ornaments: See Fig. 203. With raw edges even, pin the lace to the right side of the ornament; make a pleat at each corner or point (if applicable). Overlap the ends of the lace by about ¼ inch. Stitch the lace securely to the ornament, making a ⅛-inch seam. With right sides facing and raw edges even, stitch the ornament front to the back with the lace sandwiched in between; leave a 1½″ opening along one edge. Turn the ornament right side out through the opening, pushing out any points or corners; adjust the lace by pulling on it gently. Stuff the ornament until plump. Fold the raw edges at the opening inside and slip-stitch closed, also securing the raw edges of the lace inside. Make a loop or tie from ribbon and slip-stitch to the top or back of the ornament.

Fig. 202

Fig. 204

Stuffed plain ornaments: See Fig. 202. With right sides facing and raw edges even, stitch the ornament front to the back, leaving a 1½″ opening along one edge. Turn the ornament right side out through the opening, pushing out any points or corners. Stuff the ornament until plump. Fold the raw edges at the opening inside and slip-stitch closed. Make a loop or tie from ribbon and slip-stitch to the top of the ornament.

Stuffed bound ornaments: See Fig. 204. With raw edges even and wrong sides facing, stitch the ornament front to the back, making a ⅛-inch seam and leaving a 1½-inch opening. Stuff the ornament until plump; then stitch the opening closed. Bind the ornament as directed in *Binding a Project*. If you can, continue the binding up along one side edge for about 5″ to make the loop; stitch the end of the binding to the back of the ornament to finish the loop. Otherwise, make a separate loop; see *Loops & Ties*.

118

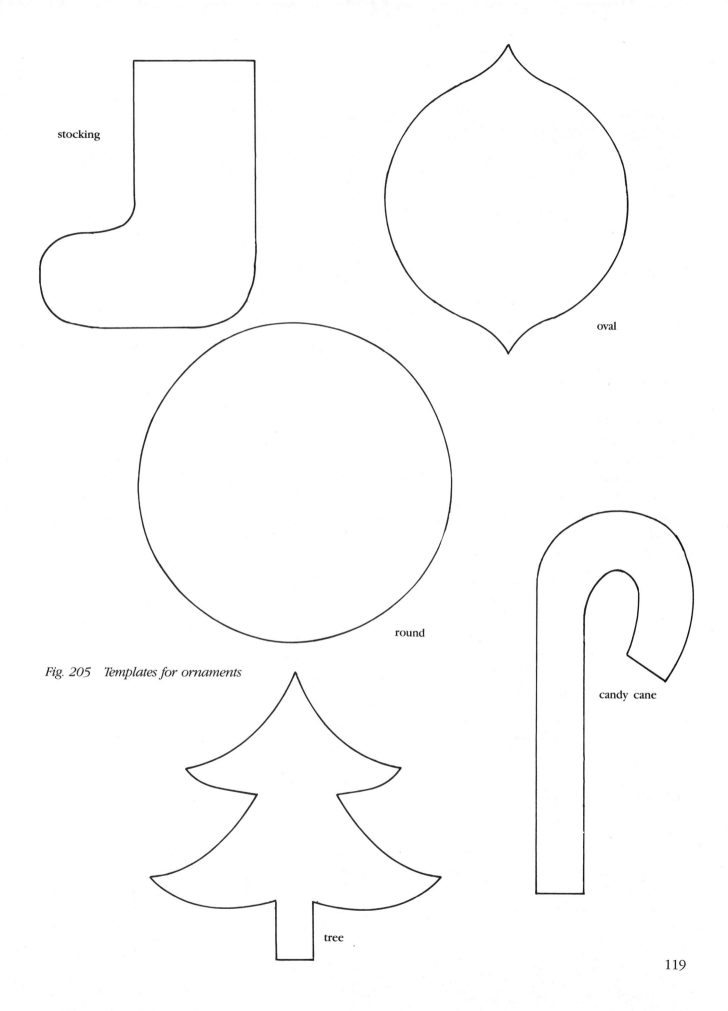

stocking

oval

round

Fig. 205   Templates for ornaments

candy cane

tree

119

INSTRUCTIONS FOR INDIVIDUAL ORNAMENTS

Round (or Oval) Ornaments: Cut a variety of strips ranging from ½ inch to 1½ inches wide. Trace the round or oval pattern and use it to cut one circle or oval from muslin or other neutral fabric. Begin in the middle by placing your first strip right side up on the right side of the muslin; pin or baste the strip in place. Place the next strip over the first strip with right sides facing and raw edges approximately matching; stitch in place along the top edge. Fold the second strip up and press. Continue adding fabric strips above and below the central strip in this manner until all the muslin is covered. If you wish to add lace to one of the fabric strips, pin the lace on top of the appropriate strip, with the top edge of the lace slightly below the raw edge of the strip; baste in place. Place the next strip on top of the lace, with right sides facing; stitch together securing the lace in the seam, fold the new strip up and press. When the ornament is covered, press carefully; then turn over to the wrong side. Trim away the uneven edges of the strips so that they are even with the edge of the muslin. Topstitch ⅛ inch away from the edge of the ornament all around. Complete the ornament by one of the methods given above.

Christmas Tree Ornament: Make as directed for the round ornament, except place your first strip at an angle as shown in the color photograph. It is probably easiest to make this ornament with a plain finish; after you have sewn the front and back together, clip into the seam allowance right to your stitching line. Leave the bottom portion of the tree unstitched for ease in turning right side out. After turning right side out, fold the raw edges at the bottom and the trunk inside and slip-stitch together by hand.

Stocking: Make as directed for the round ornament, or simply use 2 fabrics—red for the main body of the stocking and a white strip at the top for a "cuff." Complete the ornament by one of the methods given above.

Candy Cane: Trace the candy cane pattern and cut one piece from muslin or other neutral fabric. Cut strips of red and white fabric approximately 1 inch wide. Beginning at the bottom with red, stitch the strip, right side up, to the muslin. Add a white strip next, as described for the round ornament. Continue adding red and white strips alternately, angling the strips as you reach the curved top edge; see Fig. 204. Bind the ornament with red or white bias binding, easing the binding carefully around the inner curves. Stitch a binding loop to the top of the ornament.

Two-Inch-Square Ornaments: Select one of the designs given on pages 56–59; cut and piece the design as illustrated. Complete the ornament by one of the methods described above.

Ribbons & Bows Tablecloth

See color page P.

Wrapping the gifts that have been carefully chosen for family and friends is one of my favorite Christmas tasks. I love giving beautifully wrapped packages—the bigger the better! That is what gave me the idea for designing this tablecloth. It will make your table resemble a huge Christmas present, complete with ribbons and bows.

The patchwork is very simple to piece and quick to make (I cut and pieced the entire tablecloth top in about 3 days). It's all straight and easy sewing, and makes an excellent scrap project. Be bold! Choose a wild variety of fabrics for the little squares. After all, ribbons should be brightly colored.

I used batting between the pieced top and back because I like the way that batting softens the edge of a table. The project does not require batting, however, and if you are planning to use the tablecloth during meals, I would recommend only a simple lining (back).

Before beginning, review the following sections: *Assembling a Project for Quilting, How to Quilt* and *Binding a Project.*

Easy
Finished size: 60 inches square
Requirements
Pieced top: 1 yard light fabric, 1 yard bright fabric, 1¼ yards medium fabric; 144 2½" × 2½" squares—fabric scraps
Back: 2 pieces 31¼" × 62½"—3¼ yards (allows for self-binding)
Batting (optional): 61" square
Separate binding (optional): 1¼" × 244"—½ yard

Instructions: There are 280 pieces in the tablecloth top. Using the templates given here, cut the following pieces from fabric:

A	2 light	H	24 medium
B	4 medium	J	8 light
C	2 light	K	12 bright, 144 assorted
D	8 bright		
E	16 medium	L	4 medium
F	8 bright	M	8 medium
G	32 bright, 8 medium		

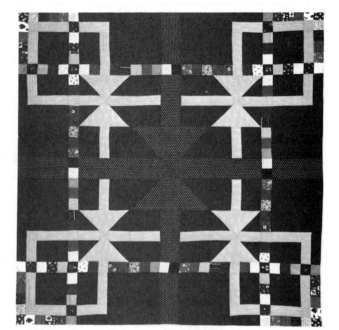

Fig. 206

Piece the tablecloth in 3 sections—the central section and the 2 outer sections. Following Fig. 207 and Fig. 208 carefully, arrange the pieces on a large flat surface. Piece the central section first, then the outer sections.

Begin the patchwork with the big central bow. Sew B to opposite sides of each A. Sew a B-A-B triangle to one side of each C, as shown in the illustrations. Matching seams carefully in the middle, sew the A-B-C triangles together.

Next, construct each small bow. Sew E to opposite sides of each D. Sew an E-D-E triangle to one side of each F, as shown in the diagram. Matching seams in the middle, sew the D-E-F triangles together, forming 4 small bows.

Construct the inner ribbon rectangles next. Sew an H to each side of 8 bright G's. Sew H-G-H to each side of 4 J's. With the J's in a horizontal position, sew a ribbon rectangle to each side of the big central bow. Sew a small bow to each side of the remaining ribbon rectangles with the J's in a vertical position. Sew the strips just made to the upper and lower edges of the central bow, matching seams carefully.

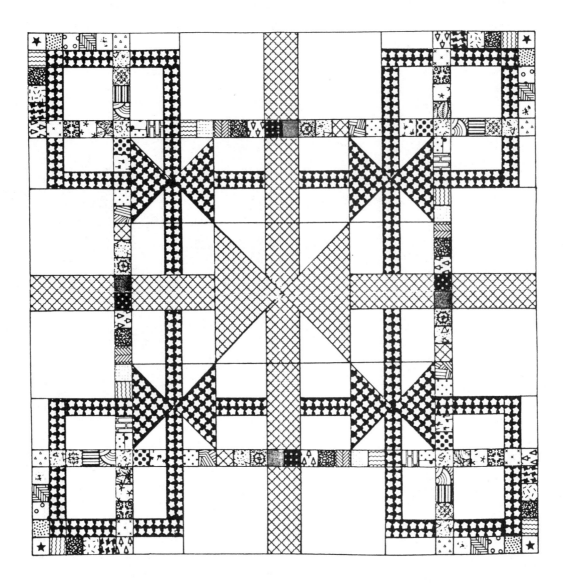

Fig. 207

Now you can construct the 4 outer ribbon rectangles, studying the illustrations carefully as you proceed. Sew an M to each side of each remaining J. Assemble 8 G-G pieces by sewing 8 medium G's to 8 bright G's. Assemble 8 G-H pieces by sewing 4 bright G's to the right edge of 4 H's and to the left edge of the other 4 H's. Sew each H-G to the bright edge of each G-G piece as shown in the diagram. Sew the rectangles just made to the side edge of each M with the bright G's touching the M's.

Next, assemble the 4 multicolor ribbon strips. Arrange 4 rows of K pieces with 18 K's in each row; a bright K should be placed in the third and sixteenth positions of each strip. When you are satisfied with the color arrangement, sew the K pieces together,

creating 4 long strips. Sew one K strip to each of the outer ribbon rectangles, forming what we'll call a multicolor ribbon rectangle. Sew a multicolor ribbon rectangle to the upper and lower edges of the central square as shown. (Set aside the other 2 multicolored ribbon rectangles for the moment.) The central section is now complete.

For each outer section, sew a light G to each L. Sew a bright G to each of the remaining bright K's; sew to each G-L with the K forming a corner between the 2 G's, as shown in the illustration. Encircle each G-K-L square with 20 K pieces as shown. When you are satisfied with the arrangement, sew the K pieces together in 2 strips of 4 and 2 strips of 6. Sew the short K strips to the upper and lower

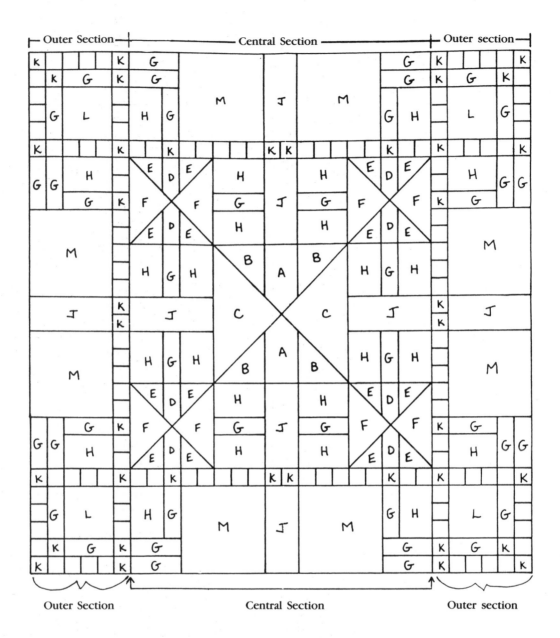

Fig. 208

edges of each G-K-L square; then sew the long K strips to each side edge.

Sew the squares just made to each end of the multicolor ribbon rectangles previously set aside, taking care to position the squares correctly for each corner, as shown in Fig. 208. Finally, sew the outer sections to each side of the central section, matching seams carefully. Your tablecloth top is now complete.

To make the back, sew the long edges of the back pieces together, making a ½-inch seam; press the seam to one side.

If you do not wish to quilt your tablecloth, pin the back to the pieced top with right sides facing; trim the back even with the top. Stitch together around all edges, making a ¼-inch seam and leaving a 3-inch opening along one edge for turning. Clip away the seam allowance at each corner at an angle; turn right side out through the opening. Fold the raw edges at the opening ¼ inch inside and slip-stitch closed. Press carefully. To secure the back to the top, topstitch ¼ inch from the outer edges all around; then topstitch along the edges of each of the ribbons, using matching thread.

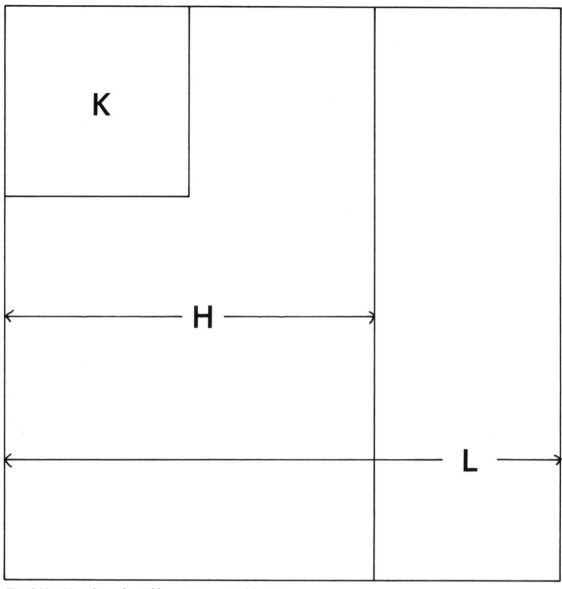

Fig. 209   *Templates for Ribbons & Bows Tablecloth*

If you wish to quilt your tablecloth, see *Assembling a Project for Quilting*. Hand- or machine-quilt the large central bow and ribbons in a diagonal checkerboard pattern; quilt the smaller bows and ribbons with parallel lines. Then quilt along the edges of the multicolor ribbons.

Fabric has been allowed for self-binding the tablecloth; if you are adding a separate binding or fold-finishing the project, trim the back so that it is even with the quilt top; then proceed. See *Binding a Project* for instructions on finishing the edges of the tablecloth; the project shown in the color photograph was fold-finished.

Variation: Make up this design in colors to match your bedroom or living room and use as a quilt.

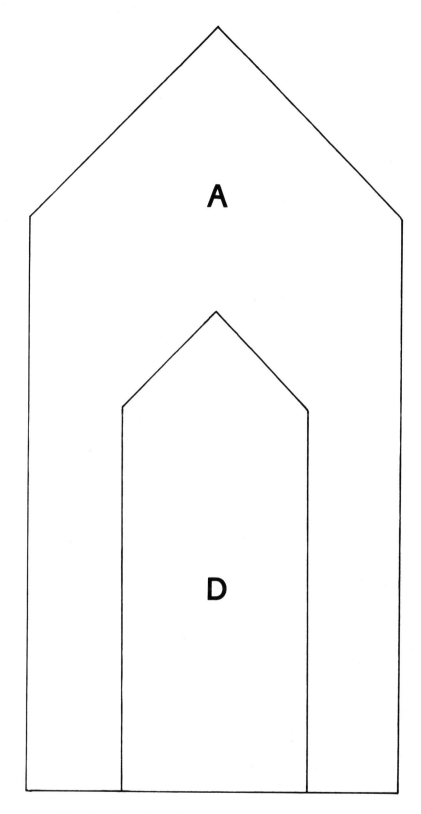

Fig. 210   Templates for Ribbons & Bows Tablecloths, continued

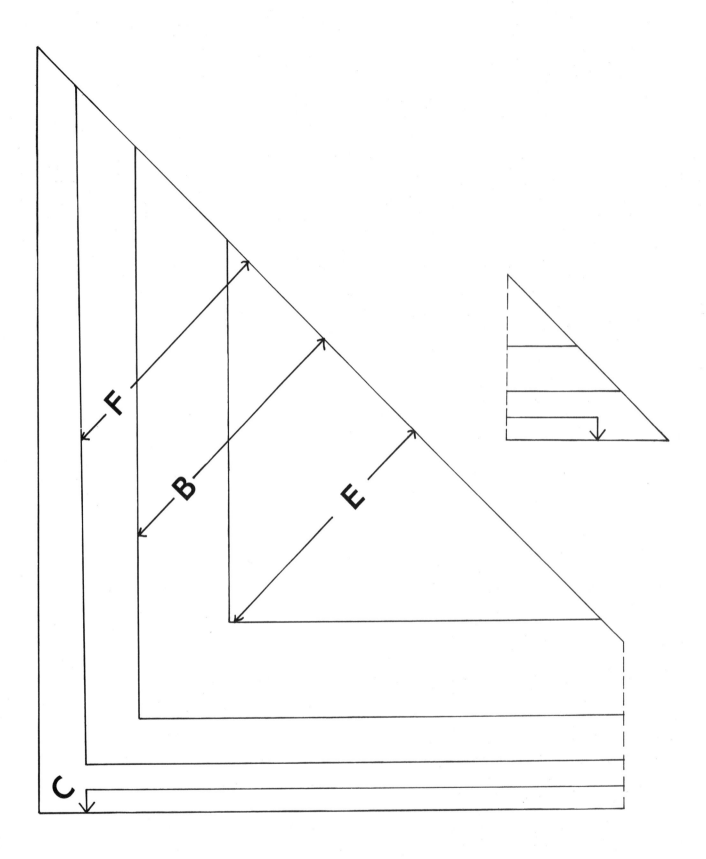

Fig. 211   Templates for Ribbons & Bows Tablecloth, continued. Trace entire triangle and place on fold for C.

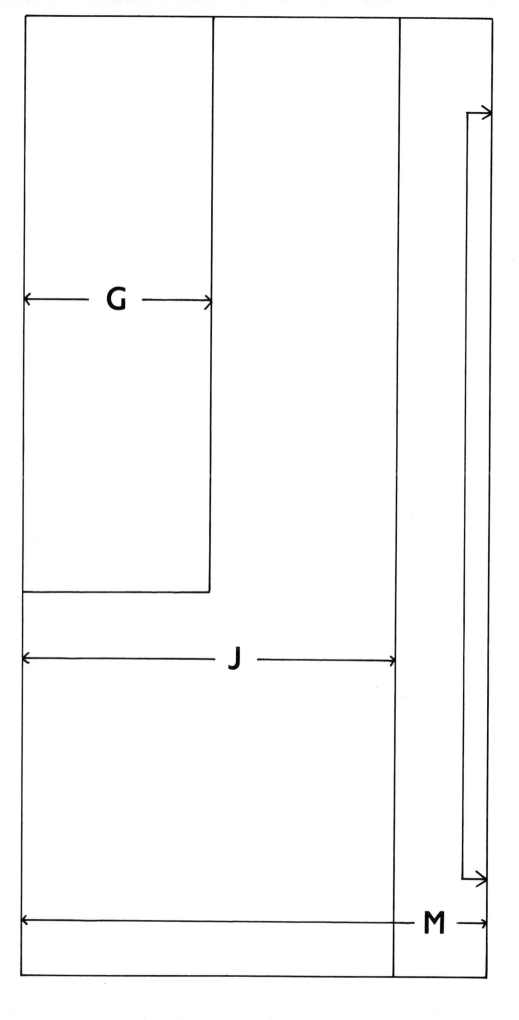

Fig. 212   Templates for Ribbons & Bows Tablecloth, continued. Trace entire rectangle and place on fold for M.

INDEX